Patrick's great contribution to the global conversation regarding work as worship is its precise and persistent application to those parts of His world where the gospel is least heard, observed, and embraced by those who have been called, chosen, and commissioned to be His witnesses to the uttermost parts of the earth. Being children of a Father for whom justice is a central character trait requires of us prompt obedience in going to the least reached, and appropriate modelling of the Kingdom in our discipling of the nations.

—Peter Shaukat, co-founder of a global investment fund focused on North Africa, the Middle East and Asia

God wants us as Christians to walk, work and worship with divine clarity and cohesiveness while living in a world of ambivalence and ambiguity. Patrick Lai's book provides the Biblical basis and substance for this in a clear and convincing fashion. It will inspire true worship.

—Lud Golz, Pastor Emeritus Fellowship Bible Church, Chagrin Ohio and Radio Bible Teacher, "Getting God's Message."

Those who lead often are too busy to write about it. But Patrick Lai has been leading the Business as Mission movement since before it was called BAM. We can all benefit from his reflections on the fundamental drivers of Kingdom work in "finishing the task". Thank you, Patrick, for work well done!

—Gary Ginter, Chairman & Co-Founder, VAST Power Systems, Inc.

WORKSHIP

WORKSHIP

RECALIBRATE WORK AND WORSHIP

PATRICK LAI

I dedicate this book to my Master, Savior, King and best friend—Jesus.
Without you, Jesus, we have no purpose in life and breath. Holy Spirit,
may this book be a helpful step for each reader in expediting Your kingdom
to come and Your will to be done on earth as it is in heaven. The first fifty
years have been terrific, Father, I look forward to the next fifty thousand.

Praise the LORD! Praise God in his sanctuary;
praise him in his mighty firmament!
Praise him for his mighty deeds;
praise him according to his exceeding greatness!
Let everything that breathes praise the LORD!
Praise the LORD!
Psalm 150:1,2,6

CONTENTS

PREFACE

This Workship Series is a culmination of what the Lord has been teaching me as I wrestled with issues related to work and worship. In 1984, after working in a church in my home culture for five years, the Lord led me to serve Him overseas. As a result, this book has an emphasis on cross-cultural mission and God's heart for all peoples. Yet, the issues addressed are relevant to all who desire to glorify Jesus wherever He has led you to work. I pray each reader will gain fresh insights into God's perspective on life and work and be challenged to live for Him as we integrate work and worship as WORKSHIP for His glory.

————

Early in his leadership of the Israeli army, Joshua encounters another warrior.

While Joshua was near Jericho, he raised his eyes and saw one who stood facing him, drawn sword in hand. Joshua went up to him and asked, "Are you one of us or one of our enemies?"[1] He replied, "Neither. I am the commander of the army of the Lord: now I have come."

Joshua assumes there are two sides in every battle, but he quickly discovers this is wrong. In Scripture, there's my side, your side and God's side. God does not take sides. He loves every human being, no matter which army or which side we choose to join.

Do you rulers indeed speak justly …[2] One of my many failings in life and certainly in the business-as-mission world has been a spirit of criticism. Yet in my studies of God's Word, I realize He has not called me to be a critic, but a witness. My assignment is not to condemn or condone the world, but to love it. And I doubt that I am alone in resembling the Pharisees of Jesus' day who sometimes lost sight of the fact that the study and interpretation of Scripture are not to be an end in itself. God has given us His written Word for a practical purpose —*That the man of God may be complete, equipped for every good work.*[3] When there is a gap between the classroom or the pulpit and the everyday life of a follower of Jesus, sterility and superficiality often fill the church.

I believe the Father has led me to write this book not to convert those who defend the status quo, but rather to rally those who are ready to challenge that status quo and replace it with a reality that is vastly more in line with what God intends for His bride—the church. This book and those that will follow are for every human being who hungers to find and fulfill our God-given, deep-seated human need to be one with Him in all that we say and do. I wrote this for those who long to see His Kingdom come and His will be done in us and through us.

The church and parachurch agencies may not yet have embraced the integration of faith and work, but they are at least shaking hands. The church for its part is still confused by the mixed messages it is hearing, but it is paying attention and seeking to understand. And at least in North America, the Christian business community is becoming informed and is pursuing discernment in how best to worship God in and through the workplace. This is encouraging. As we strive to integrate our faith and work and see all peoples bow their knees before Jesus, we are witnessing real progress.

Though there are still several barriers to overcome in the integration of faith and work including the acceptance of business as worship, and a valid strategy for winning people to Jesus—the biggest hurdle may be me, or perhaps us; those leading the business as mission (BAM) movement.

Last week I had a conversation with my younger son. He owns a small-medium enterprise (SME) in one of the most dangerous Muslim cities in the world. He pointed out to me that my generation, the first generation of BAMers (Business as Mission workers), carries a negative stigma toward mission agencies, Non-Government Organizations (NGOs) and missionaries. For twenty years Christian leaders criticized and cajoled those of us who were doing business as mission. We were repeatedly told how wrong we were to do business as a ministry. Their jabs hurt. Their punches even knocked some out of the race. They were downright nasty. Though many still do not clearly understand us, things are changing. But the millennials and especially Gen Z have not had negative experiences with traditional mission agencies that we business-as-mission-minded boomers have had. These future workers do not carry the questions and fears about BAM that the boomers and Gen X carry. However, as a result of our past hurts and old baggage, we are projecting the wrong questions and fears upon these new workers. We need to realize that many of these questions and fears do not exist for young people. The repetition of our stressful experiences is hurting, not helping. We need to forgive and forget.

Consider, when I left our first mission agency to do business, my field supervisor threatened me, "If you go into business you will never plant a church!" Clearly that's been proven wrong. The deficiencies in mission agencies have fed their own fears, but we (millennials especially) need to recognize that the mission world today is different. Yes, there are still problems—big problems. Certainly, wrong, bad, sinful attitudes prevail and we must refrain from encouraging them. We need to correct the problems and press forward. Our assignment is not to criticize, but to build one another up in love.

BAM and B4T (business for transformation) workers were misunderstood and under attack from the early days in the mid-nineteen eighties. As a result, for the first twenty-five years we played defense. As a leader in those movements, I may have been the most defensive. That said, I now want to be the first to step forward and own up to my share of the blame. Forgive me! I want to be the first to offer an olive branch of reconciliation.

> B4T – *businesses and people strategically working in an unreached area (10/40 Window) that is striving for profitability and designed to create jobs and bless the local community in Jesus' name. B4T is a subset of BAM, in that BAM is worldwide and B4T is focused on the Muslim, Hindu, and Buddhist peoples of the world.*

Reconciliation. While we do not necessarily need to partner with mission agencies, many of whom clearly do not yet understand who we are and what we do, we do need to stop criticizing both the parachurch organizations and the churches as they once criticized us. Whether they wish to own up to their lack of study or not is their problem. We need to move forward. We need to be noble, like the Bereans, and examine the Scriptures to discern His truth.[4] We need to focus on a new generation of God's people, God's workers who truly wish to integrate their faith and work. We need to stop complaining and pointing fingers at our brothers and sisters. We need to start working toward honesty, righteousness and godly attitudes and relationships.

In a *Christianity Today* article titled, "An Apology to the Christian 99%, from the 1%," Michael Oh wrote to all Christian workplace professionals stating, "*You don't exist to help professional ministry leaders fulfill the Great Commission. We exist to help you do it.*"[5]

Well said, but what has changed? We may seek reconciliation and that is good, but the problems continue to exist. To move forward in obedience to fulfilling the Great Commission, we need to address *and* solve the problems. Too often "in grace" we avoid the solutions so that we can live in harmony. However, Jesus had no problem overturning tables in the temple, nor calling the religious leaders hypocrites and telling them they were damned to hell.

Reconciliation is important, but reconciliation that is not based on truth is shallow, and reconciliation that does not involve changed behavior is hypocritical. When we set aside the root problems to focus on surface issues, we are being blind guides. Truth is the rock upon which God's church is to be built. Truth precedes harmony. Jesus is "The Truth."[6] When we build the church on harmony, that is good and right. However, if truth is not the foundation of reconciliation and we cover up or ignore problems to facilitate harmony, we are building a foundation on sand. Pope Francis stated it well when he said, *Truth may be vital, but without love it is unbearable.*

This is the first of a series of books centered on the integration of faith and work. This book focuses on the integration of *work and worship* including our "theology of work." In this first book, a biblical foundation for the integration of faith and work is laid out. All three of these books are intended to bring the problems with solutions to the forefront of the church and parachurch. Nearly all the suggested solutions have been tested and proven good, helpful and successful in bearing good fruit for the Kingdom. It does not mean that each solution is right for each organization, church or individual, and neither am I so arrogant as to posit that the ideas shared are the only one way to solve each problem. I offer these solutions as an effort to get people talking, facing our problems and biases, as to explore the reality, the truth of our lives and workship as He intends it. (Yes, *workship*—see chapter seven.) Even as God has raised up different churches and parachurches for His purposes, so He may lead each of us to apply these ideas differently.

This "workship" series of books is intended to challenge and create talking points. We need talking points. We need His wisdom and to seek His understanding. I have written this first book in an attempt to state the problems and offer biblical solutions in an attempt to bring light into our darkness of misunderstandings. And like the Bereans, I pray that each reader will prayerfully and intensely study these things to gain God's mind on them.

For those new to the missiological terms used in this book, there is a list of terms at the back of the book.

I pray this book will be a small help to you, dear reader, as we strive together in obedience to complete His Greatest Commission. I share these things not with pride, but with a sincere heart, knowing that the Lord has led me down this path.

Him we proclaim, warning every man and teaching every man in all wisdom, that we may present every man mature in Christ.—Colossians 1:28

1

RECALIBRATING

A rebel attempts to change the past; a revolutionary attempts to change the future. —Anonymous

Now that I put my hand to my head, I see there is no hat. —Persian Proverb

This is what we speak, not in words taught us by human wisdom but in words taught by the Spirit, explaining spiritual realities with Spirit-taught words. —1 Corinthians 2:13

———

AS A STUDENT at the University of Oregon, I took an Organic Chemistry class. The class required a lab portion, consisting of an experiment which, if done right, we were told, should take twenty hours. Our assignment was to blend dozens of ingredients precisely together to produce independent solutions. If each solution was perfect, mixing them together would yield the correct compound.

Well, I have never been known for being precise. And a chemist, I am not. After twenty hours I was barely halfway through the assignment. Every week I had to recalibrate my solutions to correct minuscule errors I had made. I had to recalculate and recalibrate the solutions I was mixing to ensure the percentages of each ingredient were correct. Eventually, I completed all the calibrations correctly, mixed the solutions together and achieved the desired result—a passing mark! After thirty hours of work, I called my professor to come and grade my final product. As he turned the corner into my workstation, I reached across the counter to move a Bunsen burner, only to bump the beaker containing my final compound, which sent it crashing to the floor! When I graduated three years later, there was still a huge purple mark on the floor where that beaker had burst.

Life, like chemistry, requires frequent recalibrations. Change is happening all around us, requiring us to adjust. Recalibrating regularly is essential. If we recalibrate often enough, we will never veer too far off-course.

Hindus and Buddhists have shrines in their workplaces. Islam was, and continues to be, spread by businesspeople. The Pew Research Center projects that Islam will grow more than twice as fast as the overall world population over the next three decades and will become the world's largest religious group.[1] Three of the major religions teach their followers how to integrate their lives and work better than we do. *We* separate what *they* integrate. Is it any wonder that Islam is growing faster than Christianity and that Christianity is on the decline in the West?[2]

We must make a major paradigm shift in our efforts if we are to succeed in reaching the whole world. At home and abroad our efforts are yielding far less than the 100% Jesus offers.[3] In addition, over 90% of all missionaries sent out from North America go and serve among reached people groups where churches exist. Meanwhile, those peoples and places without a witness continue to live in darkness.[4] Based on our inclination toward comfort, safety and success, it comes as no surprise that missionaries favor going where churches are well established.[5] But, Jesus conditions His return on the fact that all ethnic people in the world will have an awareness of Him—and then He will return.[6] The word most often translated as *nation* in Matthew 24:14 is the Greek word ἔθνος (ethnos). Conceptually it means *race, people, nation*. Yet most of the least-reached peoples in the world live in countries that do not grant missionary visas. Revelation 7:9 says, *"After this I looked, and there before me was a great multitude that no one could count, from every nation, tribe, people and language, standing before the throne and before the Lamb."*[7] If we are to witness to people from *every nation, tribe, people and language* worshipping Jesus, then our methods and approaches need to change. And though many countries are closed to missionary work, these same countries are wide open to doing business, even business done in Jesus' name.

Missions and the church have both been in a time warp. Fresh eyes —a new perspective is needed for sharing God's message both overseas and at home. Population explosions and economic implosions are changing the marketplace and changing communities. New infrastructures for recruiting, training, mobilizing, supporting and caring for field workers are needed—

NOW!

We need to revisit what Scripture teaches about life and work and mission. We likely have some things wrong—possibly many things. No surprise there. Jesus tells us that as we approach the end times, the majority of people claiming to be His followers will have things wrong.[8] Yet, in His grace and for His glory, we must keep pressing ahead.

Warnings

I enjoy sports and I often find humor in the enthusiasm of commentators. A favorite line that commentators of every sport use to warn us to be alert is, "This is the most important play of the game!" Obviously, this next play is the most important play of the game, as it is the play that is happening now. The plays that are completed are history; they cannot be changed. And the plays in the future will be impacted by this present play. So yes! Of course, this is the most important play of the game.

In a similar vein—be warned—getting work (our daily nine to five jobs) integrated into the church and our overseas mission work is presently the most important factor in reaching all peoples. Note, I am not saying it is *the* most important factor; rather it is the most important factor in the present. Every day that passes brings us one day closer to the Lord's return. In speaking about His return, Jesus gives us a variety of forewarnings.

"Not everyone who says to me, 'Lord, Lord,' will enter the kingdom of heaven, but only the one who does the will of my Father who is in heaven. Many will say to me on that day, 'Lord, Lord, did we not prophesy in your name and in your name drive out demons and in your name perform many miracles?' Then I will tell them plainly, 'I never knew you. Away from me, you evildoers!'" (Matthew 7:21-23)

"Because of the increase of wickedness, the love of most will grow cold." (Matthew 24:12)

"Make every effort to enter through the narrow door, because many, I tell you, will try to enter and will not be able to. Once the owner of the house gets up and closes the door, you will stand outside knocking and pleading, 'Sir, open the door for us.' But he will answer, 'I don't know you or where you come from.' Then you will say, 'We ate and drank with you, and you taught in our streets.' But he will reply, 'I don't know you or where you come from. Away from me, all you evildoers!'" (Luke 13:25-27)

A growing number of believers are heeding Jesus' warnings. They have initiated a revolution. Thousands of believers in Jesus around the world are leaving the old, historical, accepted ways of doing mission work cross-culturally for even older, more biblical paths. These people, who for Christ's sake have left the green pastures of life to traverse the narrow ravine through the valley of the shadow of death, find this hard and narrow way leads them into the heart of enemy territory—Muslim, Buddhist and Hindu strongholds. Yet sadly, there's confusion in the ranks. Who is the enemy? Those doing business cross-culturally are being attacked by the enemies' fundamentalists from the front—no surprise there—but they are also being shot at from behind by church and mission leaders!

These older approaches are rooted in God's Word. The catalyst for this transition is nothing less than expediting Jesus' condition for His return—*And this gospel of the kingdom will be preached throughout the whole world as a testimony to all nations, and then the end will come.*[9] These dutiful soldiers of Jesus' army are moving forward into the darkest corners of Satan's realm with righteousness and authenticity—being above reproach.[10]

In their book, *Pagan Christianity*, Viola and Barna research and explore the roots of church practices and highlight the new types of workers needed to reach the unreached. One key point is understanding the motivations of those who seek to integrate life and work whom they call Revolutionaries. This excellent work clarifies, "*The heart of the Revolutionaries is not in question. There is ample research to show that they are seeking more of God. They have a passion to be faithful to His Word and to be more in tune with His leading. They ardently want their relationship with the Lord to be their top priority in life. They long to think the thoughts of Jesus. They desire to make every movement with Jesus. They yearn to inhale every breath with Jesus. They hunger for a relationship with God that feeds and fills their soul. They search for like-hearted others, who recognize that same desire to go deep in Him. They are tired of the institutions, denominations, and routines getting in the way of a moment-by-moment connection with Him. They are worn out on the endless programs that fail to facilitate transformation. They are tired of reading books on discipleship when they long for a true mentor in their life. They are weary of being sent off to complete assignments, memorize facts and passages and engage in simplistic practices that do not draw them into God's presence.*"[11]

Those seeking to integrate their life and work are people who have experienced the goodness of God. They want to make a difference. They pursue truth, transparency and excellence in their life and work.

And above all else they seek a deep, intimate relationship with Jesus. Second to that, they seek righteous relationships with others. They walk by faith—not by sight—unencumbered in their life and work because Jesus is their source of sustenance.

As we see the changes and sense new opportunities, we need to revisit the past efforts, measurements and calibrations of mission. When you calibrate something, you determine, check, or rectify the gradation of the tool being used to assess or measure something. In the military, after firing a cannon, the gunner will determine where a shell exploded and then recalibrate the correct range for the next shot. *Workship* is the first book in a series of books that will call us to revisit past and present efforts of reaching the world and *recalibrate* to determine if we are on target for the 21st century.

As we once calibrated—and now recalibrate—every shot needs to be founded in God's word. And as we study the life of Jesus, we need to remember that the topic of the Kingdom of God and the theme of Jesus returning in glory is the central theme of the Gospels. In a brilliant booklet authored by J. Oswald Sanders, titled *The Certainties of Christ's Coming*, Sanders lists twenty-one "certainties" concerning Jesus' return that we may be sure of from Scripture. Sanders researches each point and concludes that twenty of these twenty-one certainties are things which God alone must do before Jesus will return. But there's one certainty, found in Matthew 24:14, which the followers of Jesus are commissioned and commanded to do. *And this gospel of the kingdom will be preached throughout the whole world as a testimony to all nations; and then the end will come.*[12]

In Matthew 24:14, the Greek word ἔθνος (ethnos) is often translated as "nations." However, the meaning of ethnos is much more specific than "nations." For example, we derive the English word "ethnicity" from *ethnos*. This word should be understood as every "ethnic group" in the world. An "ethnic group" or tribe, is very different in today's world, than the word "nations." According to the Joshua Project,[13] less than 10% of all missionary work is done among the ethnic groups that have no churches. Whether it is Satan's scheme to distract us and delay Jesus' return, or our fleshly nature has chosen a safer, wider, easier path to walk—we need to recalibrate. The point is that the foundation of our existing mission efforts is beginning to threaten the efforts to finish reaching all ethnic groups in the world with the Gospel. That foundation upon which we have built overseas missions—namely the professional missionary and the status she or he has in the church—is drawing people away from the least reached and more dangerous areas and into safer and easier missionary assignments. Our priorities and energies are misaligned with God's. The Great Commission is an assignment to reach all peoples with the Good News. Therefore, the church's primary focus should be to prioritize sending laborers into those places where there are few or no churches or laborers.

Here is a challenging idea. If everyone reading this book took Matthew 24:14 seriously and responded to Jesus' challenge of reaching every tribe, language, people and nation, we could finish the task of worldwide evangelization in our own generation and personally witness the Lord's return.[14] If Jesus is delaying His return for the evangelization of the world, why are we delaying reaching out to all ethnic groups? To think that a city, not to mention a country, is closed to the Gospel is absurd. At this very moment there are Christian businesspeople working in every country of the world. No land, no country, no government is closed to profitable, job-creating, tax-paying, government-honoring business. The fact is, there are no closed doors to the Gospel. There are, however, disobedient followers. Many followers seem to have counted the cost and determined that He is NOT worth the perceived risk.[15] Rather than pursue taking Jesus' glory to all the world, we argue about the definition of words such as ethos, and we debate the details of eschatology.

Some might ask, "How are we to know when all peoples have heard the Gospel? How will we know when His mission is completed?" God knows exactly who "all nations" are. Both Matthew 24:36 and Acts 1:7 point out that no one knows the times and dates the Father has set for Jesus' return.[16] We aren't supposed to know. The single most important thing we need to know is that our assignment is not yet complete. Our responsibility is to execute His task; not exegete it. Until Christ's return, our work is undone. And only God Himself understands what that looks like.

In the late 1800s, many people dubbed western Africa as "The white man's graveyard." Hundreds of missionaries died in their attempts to evangelize the hundreds of unreached ethnic groups there. Diseases like Typhoid, Yellow Fever and Malaria claimed so many lives that some missionaries from America packed and shipped their possessions to Africa in their own coffins. Family, personal safety and sacrifice paled in comparison to these missionaries' love for Jesus. They counted the cost and were happily willing to pay it.

We count the cost today too, but most are unwilling to pay it. Many go so far as to say, "Since the door is closed to missionaries, it must not be God's timing for the Gospel in that country." As well-meaning as these people are, they are mistaken. Those who cling to and wish to build on the old missionary foundation are failing to engage those ethnic groups that are still unengaged by the Gospel. In Romans 15:20-21, Paul writes, " … *thus making it my ambition to preach the gospel, not where Christ has already been named, lest I build on another man's foundation, but as it is written, 'They shall see who have never been told of him, and they shall understand who have never heard of him.'"* Sadly, these days our priorities seem to be hinged on safety, not sacrifice, and on choice, not commitment.

In recalibrating, it is fair to ask, *"If multiple churches exist in a city, is there really a need for more missionaries? Can't the Holy Spirit guide the local believers into Jesus' truth[10] as well as a missionary?"* If we answer *no* and *yes* to these two questions, then why are the majority of new missionaries being sent to places where churches already exist?

There has been an upheaval in the world requiring us to fix the foundation of world evangelization before we can live in its house again. We have reached the physical and metaphorical limits of building upon the old foundation and we need something new. The world's population will grow from the nearly 7 billion people today to a projected 9.7 billion by 2050. A much more important statistic is that we will go from a world population in which roughly one billion people have been living an "American" lifestyle, to a world in which three billion people are living at that level or aspiring to do so. "This is the first time in human history that economic growth has become the prerogative of most people on the planet."[17] The Population Reference Bureau (PBR) reports that nearly two-thirds of the Middle East's population is under the age of twenty-five and that more than one in four are unemployed.[18] Many of these frustrated, unemployed youth are finding succor in faith—Islam, Hinduism or Buddhism. These young people have a hunger and thirst for truth. They place a high value on righteousness and integrity. They seek hope and opportunities for a better life. Business, done to the glory of God, provides a key to open the door for these young people to come to Jesus.

In the past, mission agencies have played a huge role in reaching the world. We should all be extremely grateful to those who have gone before us. However, the world is changing rapidly, and yet the strategies we keep putting forward to reach Hindus, Muslims and Buddhists look a lot like the missiological strategies of the previous centuries. Yet we need to look deeper into Scripture to rediscover God's wineskins for doing His work in the present. We still need the same commitment and sacrifice—the same love for Jesus and the people being reached; but we need to recalibrate!

Business—A Solution

In the past twenty years we have moved solidly from the modern world into the postmodern world. We have gone from the 20th century to the 21st. Missions in the 21st century cannot be built on the foundations of the 19th and 20th centuries.

Change is hard. Paradigm shifts are exciting to read about in history, but they are never easy to live through. In the 1940s after World War II, GIs got a vision for going back overseas with the Gospel, instead of with guns. At that time, there was an emphasis in missions on discipleship. The Navigators, New Tribes and others came into being due to the impact of the war. In the 1960s there was the youth movement, and due to short-term mission trips YWAM (Youth With A Mission) and OM (Operation Mobilization) became popular. In the 1980s, Frontiers, Pioneers, Mission to Unreached Peoples and various other organizations started up as the emphasis began to focus on the unreached and planting churches. Each of these periods in history gave us another piece of the puzzle to God's solution for seeing His Kingdom come, His will being done, on earth as it is in heaven. I believe He is presently showing us yet another piece of the puzzle; that of business or the workplace.

God's assignment for us is to reach every tribe, language, people and nation.[19] Business opens doors into tribes, languages, peoples and nations that are closed to other strategies. Business is an old approach to sharing the Gospel; remember Paul? Today business offers new solutions—in that marketplace professionals may go places that mission agencies cannot, namely Muslim, Hindu and Buddhists regions where there are few or no churches.

By definition, business is a money-making organization. For believers, there's the added purpose of being a blessing to others. Steven, an OPEN[20] network coach to B4T[21] businesses, teaches, "Yes we need to make money. If we don't make money, we won't have a business. As Christian businessmen and women, we need to understand that along with making money, we are to be witnesses and a blessing to our employees, our suppliers, our customers and our community."

"Real business. Real impact." This is the tagline for the OPEN Network, a network of over one hundred and twenty businesses that prioritize working where there are few or no churches. Godly business, done in an ungodly environment, often results in encounters with Jesus. Profitable, scalable business done God's way—with excellence and righteousness—leads to natural opportunities to share the Good News.

Summary

This is the first in a series of books that will focus on areas which need to be recalibrated. The series will show how business has an answer to nearly every roadblock that governments and Muslim, Buddhist and Hindu fundamentalists throw at the Gospel. Whether you are in Timbuktu or Tampa, working alongside people in the marketplace creates opportunities to serve and love people. People and governments welcome good business. We need to return to the ways of the early apostles and work with our own hands.[22]

One faculty that distinguishes humankind from the animal world is our ability to imagine and dream. We need to shed our metaphorical boxes and imagine and dream. Yes, we are dreaming great dreams— His dreams. And yes, our expectations are as high as the heavens. We believe this is of God. The results are coming in. Engaging the unengaged in the workplace contextualizes us in a way that no other missionary strategy can. Working side by side with people enables them to see Jesus in us. Seeing is believing.

John teaches us that words are important, but actions are of greater importance.[23] Consider how many times you've heard the following phrases:

"Talk is cheap."
"He talks the talk, but he doesn't walk the walk."
"Actions speak louder than words."

James adds, *"What good is it, my brothers and sisters, if someone claims to have faith but has no deeds?"*[24]

Recalibrating is not about destroying missions as they exist today. Rather, it is about doing what is right to expedite the day when every knee will bow and every tongue will confess that Jesus is the King of Kings. However, I want to be clear that this is how God worked in my life and this is the message that He has given me to share. It should not be viewed as prophecy or a one-size-fits-all recipe for reaching the nations.

These books are an effort to explain the issues and concerns about current mission practices and to offer tested, righteous, Christ-centered solutions. This book is meant to be the opening salvo in the revolution by pointing out that at this moment in history, BAM is the most important play in God's plan for reaching the world. I hope that others will follow up with their stories and experiences. The pieces of God's puzzle are coming together. We are constructing a picture of the pure glory of Jesus Christ moving deeper into the least-reached corners of the world. The most effective way to engage the unengaged is to have believers working together and recognizing that every one of us has a role, even—or *especially*—those working in the marketplace.

My prayer is that these books will challenge the way you see the world and your work in it. I hope it encourages you in your walk with Jesus and shakes up your paradigms of "what is *ministry*."

Let's start recalibrating.

2

WHY WE DO BUSINESS
SUE'S STORY

A business that makes nothing but money is a poor kind of business.
—Henry Ford

People don't care how much you know until they know how much
you care. —Theodore Roosevelt

In the same way, let your light shine before others, that they may see your
good deeds and glorify your Father in heaven. —Jesus

———

IN 1999 WE opened three businesses. We had one team member who
had a master's degree and plenty of experience working in IT. We had
a second team member who had a master's degree in teaching English
as a second language. Together we wrote a business plan and took out
a bank loan to open one business that taught English and offered
computer services. However, in applying for permits with the government we were told that we had to open two businesses, as a language
school must be registered under the Ministry of Education and an IT

business must be registered under the Ministry of Trade and Development. We did not have enough money to have two separate facilities. So to provide one common working space for the two businesses, we also opened a business center—a co-working space. The business center enabled us to rent office space back to the two businesses while having only one secretary, one fax machine, etcetera, all in one office.

A few weeks before the grand opening, we knew we needed someone to manage all three businesses. After numerous interviews, I hired Sue to manage them. Sue was my first local hire. In hiring Sue and with everyone else we hired, I made it clear to them—whether Muslim, Hindu, Christian or Buddhist—that we run our businesses according to the principles of the Bible and if that is a problem, they might not want to work for us.

Sue took the job and started immediately as the manager overseeing all three businesses. After she had worked with us for about a week, together we had hired eight other people to work under her: four Muslims, two Buddhists and two local Christians. In preparing the businesses to open, I asked Sue to put together a marketing plan to promote the language school within the community.

Several days later she came back to me with a very nicely typed plan in a manila folder and said, "Mr. Patrick, please read this through and then let me know what you think we should do."

I took the plan, looked at her and said, "Sue, let me pray about it and then I'll let you know what we should do." Sue looked at me kind of funny, but because I was the boss, she didn't say anything. I then asked the Lord about the plan and got back to her.

I made it my discipline that whenever Sue or anyone asked me for input, I would respond, "Let me pray about it and then I'll tell you what we should do." After a few weeks it became kind of a joke around the office. Sue and others would give me things for a decision and say, "Mr. Patrick, I have something for you to pray about." Then they would smile or chuckle. Despite the teasing, I knew they were getting the point that this wasn't my business; it was God's business and I wanted it to run His way.

Sue was a great manager; she did everything with excellence. I could not have asked for a finer employee. Our office opened at 8:30AM, six days a week. Initially we taught four languages. Our classes usually started at 9AM, with business clients arriving at various times. Sue opened the office each morning and I would usually get there about 8:45AM. By then, Sue and everyone else would already be at their workstations. One morning after Sue had worked for me for about a year, I arrived as usual and found everyone standing outside. Sue wasn't there. I asked where Sue was, but nobody knew. I opened up the building, let everybody in, and went to my desk. No sooner had I sat down when Sue came rushing in, totally discombobulated.

Obviously, there was a problem. I walked over and asked her, "What's the matter?"

Without looking up she nonchalantly answered, "Oh nothing."

I replied, "Well, something's the matter. You've never been late before. What happened? Did you have a flat tire?"

"No, no," she said, revealing a bit of anxiety. "Everything's fine."

I pressed in. "Come on Sue, what's the matter? Why are you late?"

Now full of consternation she looked up and quietly exclaimed, "Ian's sick." Ian is her eight-year-old son.

I quickly extended my sympathy, "I'm so sorry. May I pray for him?"

By now prayer was something that we had worked into our office culture. It was not unusual for me to pray for problems—personal or work related both privately at employee's workstation as well as in group meetings.

Though Sue was a strong Buddhist who had two Buddhist altars in her home, she looked at me with anxious eyes and said, "Yes, please." I stood there in her office and prayed for her son Ian. After I finished praying, I began to walk out.

As I was walking out, the Lord put a thought in my mind so I turned to her and asked, "So who's taking care of Ian? Your mother?"

Sue responded, "No, my mother's out of town."

I stopped walking. Again, I pressed in, "So did your husband stay home from work?"

"No, he has a big project that's due the end of the week."

I knew in the local culture that you do not let just anyone watch your children. In fact, it is rare to allow anyone who's not a relative to take care of your children. So, I continued, "Sue, then who's taking care of Ian?"

Tears were now forming in her eyes. "Nobody," she said.

I turned fully to face her and said with less sensitivity than intended, "Are you telling me that Ian is home all alone and he's sick?"

"Yes," she blurted out.

I said, "Well, Sue, you need to go home and take care of him."

She quickly replied, "I can't."

"Yes, you can," I said. "I give you permission."

"No, I can't."

"It's ok," I insisted.

Again she firmly answered, "I can't."

And again I asserted, "Sue, I'm giving you permission. Go home and take care of Ian."

Gaining her composure, she urged, "You don't understand."

Trying to show empathy, I softly yet quickly responded, "I guess I don't understand. Why can't you go home?"

She looked at me and stated, "I cannot go home because you have put me in charge of all your businesses. Everyone looks up to me. As the manager, I am next to you. I have used all of my vacation and all of my sick leave for this year. If I cheat on the system, everyone else will expect to be able to cheat on the system too." Then with firmness she added, "I cannot go home."

Now that shows you how righteous and honest she is. Nonetheless, I pushed. "Sue, I understand that. It's okay. Go home."

She shook her head for emphasis and exhorted, "No! You don't understand how things work in this country! I really cannot go home!"

Looking her straight in the eyes I said, "Sue, if you do not go home right now I'm going to fire you."

Her whole demeanor changed. Shock came over her as she sized me up and said, "You wouldn't."

I smiled a loving smile and reminded her, "You know I always keep my word."

She relaxed, and a terse smile formed on her lips. Then she picked up her purse and sped out the door.

It turned out that Ian was very sick. In fact, he had a 105-degree Fahrenheit temperature. Sue took him to a clinic and he was admitted to the hospital for nine days. During that time, my wife and I visited Ian almost every day. We often took him little gifts or a candy bar, something to encourage him. We would always pray for him as well.

Fast forward another year. One afternoon I asked Sue to do something for me. When I asked, she looked at me kind of funny but didn't say anything. About an hour later she came into my office with Don, one of our Western co-workers.

Don asked me, "Did you ask Sue to do this?"

"Yes," I replied.

"Well," he continued, "did you know this is illegal in this country?"

Surprised, I retorted, "No. It's not illegal in the United States."

"Well, it is illegal here," he countered, chagrined that I would contemplate breaking a law.

I turned to Sue and asked, "Sue, is that right? Is this illegal?"

"Yes," she said quietly as if she had done something wrong.

I lowered my voice and spoke, "Sue, you know we don't do things that are illegal. Why would you consider doing it?"

She continued to look at the floor and said, "Well, you're the boss. We do what you tell us to do."

"But Sue," I interrupted, "we don't do anything illegal."

Agitated with my abruptness she continued, "I know, that's why I asked Don what I should do."

"You did the right thing in asking Don," I encouraged her.

I had been sitting down so I stood up at that point, turned to Sue and said, "Sue, I know you don't understand this, but my book teaches that if I ask somebody to do something that is illegal, that is a sin. I have sinned against you and so I need to ask you to forgive me for asking you to break the law. Will you forgive me?"

Sue immediately turned and headed out of my office.

I called her back, she took two steps back into my office. "Sue," I repeated. "I need to know you forgive me for asking you to do this. Do you forgive me?"

Again, without a word she turned to head out the door.

A third time I called her back. She turned inside the doorway, glanced a look at me and quickly moved her eyes away.

"Sue, this is important to me," I stated as humbly as I could. "I need to know you forgive me for what I did."

Without looking up, she swung her hand at me and quickly exclaimed, "I forgive you!" She hurried out of the doorway and went down the hall. Don and I looked at one another and I decided that was good enough. She had forgiven me.

Why would Sue behave like that? Any Asian would understand — Sue was trying to save face. Not her face, but my face. In Asia, the boss never humbles himself before an employee. In fact, rarely does a boss admit to making mistakes. Sue was trying to protect and honor me.

Over the years Sue witnessed my life and the lives of the team members like Don, who were devoted to honoring Jesus. She had no choice but to see our attempts to work in the office day-in-and-day-out with Jesus. Yes, we made mistakes, but when we did, we owned those mistakes. And when we offended people, we were quick to ask forgiveness.

In addition, Sue knew we lived very simply. She, along with our employees, worked with us to both donate funds and do service projects in the community. She learned why I drove a very simple car, a van actually. Once she got upset with me concerning that van because she had been to a training seminar for office managers that day and the managers had discussed what kind of car their bosses drove. Many drove Mercedes or BMWs. When they asked Sue, "What kind of car does your boss drive?" she was embarrassed to say, "My boss has a van."

She scolded me about getting a better car. I said to her, "What kind of car do you think Jesus would drive? I mean, he didn't even have a donkey. But if he did have a car, I think He would have a big bus, probably a big yellow bus, because He traveled with so many people. Maybe," I teased, "I should get a bus."

With some panic she then urged, "No, no, just stick with the van."

Sue also saw how we held things with an open hand, allowing others to borrow our things, including the van. In addition to eight locals, we had three Westerners, all strong Christians working for us. Sue saw how all the believers helped clean the toilets and pick up garbage, jobs that only the janitor should do. Seeing the different ways we lived and worked, the priority of loving first and making money second, stirred up her curiosity. She began to realize people were more important than money. Serving, not bossing, was Jesus' way to lead a business.

Let's fast forward again another few months. At the end of every month, Sue and I would go downstairs to a Japanese restaurant on the ground floor for lunch. The owners of the restaurant knew us well and always gave us a table in the corner where we could have a working lunch. Sue and I would review the performance of all of our employees. We would review who needed a raise, who needed some more training and who needed to be fired. We would review the month's work of our now sixteen full-time and many of our twenty-two part-time employees.

On that day as we were reviewing the employees, we came to the assistant manager, Ramah, a devoted Muslim.

When we came to Ramah, Sue said, "I think we need to fire Ramah." I asked why and she replied that we had given him several training opportunities and he kept underperforming. Sue suggested we hire somebody new. I told Sue that I disagreed. I felt he just needed more guidance and time. Ramah had a good heart and a good attitude.

Sue agreed, but she was quick to point out that he still couldn't do his job with excellence.

I said to her, "Sue, I think we need to extend Ramah some grace."

She looked me in the eye and said with a bit of disgust, "You Christians and your grace."

I asked Sue, "Do you know what grace is?"

She replied, "Of course I do. You've told me several times."

"Well," I said, "allow me to remind you again what grace is." And for at least the third time, I shared with her about the grace of Jesus and how, because of His willingness to extend grace to us, we have an everlasting relationship with God.

After I finished, Sue looked at me and asked, "Can we get back to work now?" So, we resumed reviewing the rest of the employees. After we finished the list of names, we went back up to the office and to our respective desks.

At the end of each month, after we complete the review of all our staff, I write everyone's paycheck. That same day after my lunch discussion with Sue, I began to write the monthly checks and bonus checks. I came to Sue's name. As I paused, the Lord put an idea in my head. It's very common for me to give bonuses to our employees, usually the equivalent of five to ten US dollars. However, if somebody does something exceptional, I will give the equivalent of one hundred dollars and very rarely two hundred dollars. That day, when I came to Sue's name, the Lord put in my head to give Sue a bonus. So, I started to write ten dollars and He said very clearly, "More." I then thought of fifty dollars. "No, more." At this point I asked the Lord, "Ok, one hundred dollars?" "No, more." Then I asked Him, "Two hundred dollars?" Silence. I felt He was good with that, so I wrote Sue a bonus check for two hundred dollars.

When I have finished writing all the checks for the month, our routine is for Sue to take all the pay envelopes and distribute them to the employees. This time, after she finished, as expected, she came and sat down at her desk. Her office was across the hall from mine so I could see her chair if I left my door open. My door was open, so I watched her as she sat down and opened her pay envelope. She pulled out her paycheck and then she saw a second check, a bonus check. She took it out of the envelope, glanced at it, smiled and quickly got up and began to walk toward my office. I immediately turned my chair to face the wall.

Sue came into my office and asked, "Mr. Patrick, thanks for the bonus. What did I do to deserve this?" (The employees always ask that question because they want to do it again.)

I continued to look at the wall and I said softly, "Nothing."

She repeated herself. "Mr. Patrick, what did I do to deserve this bonus?"

I kept looking at the wall and said louder, "Nothing." We joke around a lot in our office, so Sue pressed in.

"Seriously, what did I do?" At that point I turned around and looked at her.

I said, "Sue, do you remember our discussion about grace a little while ago?"

She smiled and said, "Yeah."

"Well," I replied, "you really didn't do anything to deserve this bonus. This is God's grace to you." At that moment she kind of froze and I could see she was thinking this through in her head. Then after an awkward moment, she hurried out of my office. That was Friday afternoon.

Monday morning after I arrived at my desk, Sue came into my office and sat down. Though she often came into my office, she rarely sat down unless I invited her to do so, so I knew something was bothering her.

After a long pause, she said to me. "Mr. Patrick, can you get me a copy of your book? I would like to read it."

And so, Sue began reading the Bible. After a few weeks she began reading with one of the women who was part of our team. Then after reading with her for almost a year, Sue professed Christ as her Savior. About a year after that, we had the honor of watching Ian and his sister, Sue and her husband, all were baptized.

This is what B4T is all about. We enjoy running businesses. We like being paid for our services. We get pleasure when we create jobs that give better opportunities for people to grow and have a better life. But Sue and her family coming to know Jesus, *this is why we do business*, this is why we do anything—to glorify God.

3

RECALIBRATING OUR APPROACHES TO PEOPLE

If the people of God are to be freed for ministry in the workplace, worship will need to be viewed as involving the whole of life and not just Sunday morning. —Martin Luther

This is to my Father's glory, that you bear much fruit, showing yourselves to be my disciples. —Jesus

———

IN THE BEGINNING, before the Fall, the world was as much a spiritual place as a physical place. God was openly observable in all things. In the beginning, God's Spirit within us was the dominant force in the world. When we sinned, our human faculties of reason and emotion became the dominant force. Sin dethroned the Spirit, so our minds and emotions reigned. Jesus returned His Spirit to the throne and birthed the Church—His Bride. Yet, though we agree His Spirit is on the throne, so much of what we do in the church and the parachurch is based on knowledge or intellect. God's active grace in our lives restores the Spirit to His intended place of leadership and rule within us.

Consider the word "theology." The majority of what we do in the church centers around theology. Weekly or more, Christian leaders ask one another, "What's your theology on _____?" And the question seems to be asked in all seriousness, as if the respondent's answer will make or break the hope of further discussion. A common meaning of the word "theology" is "the study of God." Have we ever stopped to ask God what He thinks of all this studying we do of Him? We do not seem to understand that we are not created to merely *study* God. I do not believe it is His intent that we dissect every pen stroke of every letter of every word in every sentence He writes to us. Rather, we are to know God, to love God, and to serve God. We are to be in relationship with God.[1]

Solomon, the wisest man who ever lived wrote, *Be warned: the writing of many books is endless [so do not believe everything you read], and excessive study and devotion to books is wearying to the body.*[2] And to continue deemphasizing head knowledge—the mind—in the very next verse he stresses, *When all has been heard, the end of the matter is: fear God [worship Him with awe-filled reverence, knowing that He is almighty God] and keep His commandments, for this applies to every person.*[3] Paul, who himself had a great education,[4] adds, *We all possess knowledge. But knowledge puffs up while love builds up. Those who think they know something do not yet know as they ought to know. But whoever loves God is known by God.*[5] Knowledge—knowing about someone—does not necessarily lead to a relationship. I may study all about Donald Trump, but that does not mean I "know" the man. *But whoever loves God is known by God.* Love and loving someone require a relationship.

As I have grown in my relationship with Jesus, it has become clearer why Paul tells us that it is *with fear and trembling* that we are to be *working out our salvation.*[6] Let's face it, within our own thinking, it is much easier to walk by sight than it is to walk by faith. But to walk by sight is not our calling. Because when we walk by sight, we can do so with our own strength and ability. In truth we are telling God,

"Holy Spirit, You can stand aside; I can see where I am going, so You are not needed." But unless we walk by faith, we cannot please God and we have no assurance of receiving His reward.[7]

His assignment for each of us is to faithfully, daily, struggle obediently to *walk in the Spirit*.[8] We are created to seek, to behold, to love, and to experience the dominance of Jesus' Spirit in all that we are. We need to approach our lives and plan each day expecting God's empowerment to free us to live in the realm of the supernatural without our own efforts. This overrules strategies, planning, even theology if we get it right. This means ...

To pick up and embrace the cross, enduring whatever that may bring.

To be washed thoroughly in His blood: to bask in the freedom and cleansing of His sacrifice of forgiveness.

To experience full surrender, taking every thought captive to Him.[9]

To seek first to live and to breathe in the fullness of anointing and power of the Holy Spirit, that our hearts may overflow with Jesus!

Discovering, learning His way, is a mystery.[10] Yet to seek and to know Him and His righteousness is His way of unravelling the mystery.[11] *When I was a child, I talked like a child, I thought like a child, I reasoned like a child. When I became a man, I put the ways of childhood behind me*.[12] Do we accept the Scriptures with the faith of a child?[13] Or do we overcomplicate it? Over the years, through my studies, experiences and research, I have realized that God did not intend faith to be complicated. Ultimately, we are to obediently take the infallible, inerrant Scriptures at face value as God's Word.

I fully recognize my viewpoint is from that of seeing dimly in a mirror.[14] Yet when I study the relationship between the religious leaders and God in Jesus' day, I dare to ask the question, "To God, how much like the Pharisees are we—Christian leaders and myself—

today?" I also wonder, have the church and the parachurch agencies become blind guides? Are we hindering the work of God as much as spreading it? Are we justified even in asking these questions?

In the 1890s, Reverend Charles Sheldon preached to his Topeka, Kansas church a series of sermons based on the theme, "What Would Jesus Do?" Each sermon focused on various persons working in the town and applied the question, "What would Jesus do?" in their daily life and work. In his preaching and the subsequent best-selling book, *In His Steps*, Sheldon challenges us not to do anything for a whole year without first asking, "What Would Jesus Do?" One hundred years later this idea spawned the WWJD (**W**hat **W**ould **J**esus **D**o?) movement. In the book, Sheldon looks at the lives and jobs of various townspeople, including a teacher, newspaper editor and a businessman. Focusing on WWJD as a businessman, Sheldon answers the question, "What would Jesus do if He were a businessman?" with six guidelines:

1. *He [Jesus] would engage in the business first of all for the primary purpose of making money.*
2. *All money that might be made he would never regard as his own, but as trust funds to be used for the good of humanity.*
3. *His relations with all the persons in his employ would be the most loving and helpful. He could not help thinking of all of them in the light of souls to be saved. This thought would always be greater than his thought of making money in the business.*
4. *He would never do a single dishonest or questionable thing or try, in even the remotest way, to take advantage of anyone else in the same business.*
5. *The principle of unselfishness and helpfulness in the business would direct all its details.*
6. *Upon this principle he would shape the entire plan of his relations to his employees, to the people who were his customers and to the general business world with which he was connected.*[15]

Every one of these points is important. They have been central in my own business operations.

God gave us business to generate money for the individuals who work in the business (salaries to feed/house/care for families), and for the community (taxes, gifts, etcetera). Though there are many other godly functions that business serves, Sheldon correctly lists profits first. Profitability—making money—should be the number one priority in our God-honoring decision-making when at work. Why? Without profit, we have no business. The definition of a business is *a profit-making entity* or *the work of buying or selling products or services for money*.[16] So, if making a profit is the purpose of business and if Jesus is working in a business, then He will earn money better than anyone else.

Christ is the foundation stone of our work and business. Profit is the infrastructure upon which the business succeeds or fails. Without profit we have something other than a business: a charity, a club, a fellowship, even an NGO. *Whatever you do, work at it with all your heart, as working for the Lord, not for human masters.*[17] Therefore, my work is to be done first and foremost for the glory of Jesus. My work, if it is a business, should fulfill its purpose, which is to honor the Lord by making money. If I tell people, "I am in business," but I'm not making a profit, then I am not doing good business, which means my work is dishonoring God. Everything we do is to be done to God's glory.

God tells us He created us to be fruitful and multiply.[18] Jesus repeats this command in John 15 when He says we are chosen to bear fruit. Fruit-bearing encompasses all areas of our lives, including the workplace. Business is created to be profitable, so an unprofitable business is fruitless. Note: Sheldon points out in the above list that the money Jesus would make is not to line His own pockets or build Himself a huge mansion or buy a lot of toys for Himself. The money we earn, everything we own, is to be submitted to Jesus. Therefore, the money we make is to be invested first and foremost in God's purposes and not our own. Our objective in doing business is both to glorify

God and to make money so as to bring God and His transforming power into the lives of everyone who has dealings with the business. Jesus tells us, *make friends for yourselves by means of unrighteous mammon, so that when it fails, they may receive you into the eternal habitations.*[19]

Flourishing Requires Funding

Some reading this may not understand the impact of business, so I'll compare running a business with operating a church or an NGO. Both businesses and NGOs provide needed services to their communities and both need an income stream to survive. NGOs by definition are "not for profit."[20] It is the source of revenue and payment to investors that distinguishes the two. NGOs are supported at least in part by donations, whereas businesses earn their income solely from what they are paid for the services and products they offer. The objective of any one NGO may vary from healing the sick (through a clinic or hospital), feeding the hungry, providing shelter, educating children, or winning souls and discipling believers through a church. All are worthy, Biblical and God-honoring goals and objectives. Yet, understand, just as churches and NGOs are designed to bless others by fulfilling a needed purpose, businesses bless investors, but also others by fulfilling a needed purpose too. The goal of business is to make money and these monies are part of the blessing a business brings to individuals and communities. In addition, without businesses, there are no jobs and without the income from a job, people go hungry, become homeless, cannot buy medicines, and cannot send children to school.

In addition, businesses also provide products and services that people and communities want. Fulfilling the needs and wants of people and the community is an additional blessing of working in a business. Christian businesses, along with churches and NGOs, are fulfilling God's intended objectives—all are serving the community and meeting needs and wants—in the name of Jesus. Plus, along with these two blessings, the workplace provides an excellent environment for modeling and sharing the Good News. We are to interact with God and talk about God in our workplace just as we do at church and at home. The workplace may be a place of worship where we express the compassion of Christ in word and deed.

Churches, NGOs and businesses alike should be designed to glorify God and to draw people to Him. Like different parts of the body, we bless God in different ways. Sadly, businesses and sometimes even churches and NGOs are used for selfish, personal means. The misuse of business for personal gain may be more obvious than it is for NGOs, churches or other organizations, yet any organization can be corrupt. Knowing this, we cannot ignore that business and the monies businesses generate give life to the community and therefore should figure prominently in Jesus' plan to serve humanity.

Before sin came into the world, God created man for two purposes: to be fruitful and multiply and to work.[21] Profits are the fruit of doing good business. The profitability of a business is one of the many ways a business brings glory to Jesus. It is the business owner's duty to ensure that the business is conducted in ways that will glorify Him. The times that we have lost money due to poor choices or a lack of wisdom, I have asked God to forgive me for dishonoring His name. Profitability, or as Sheldon puts it, "making money," IS the primary purpose of doing business. If a business is not making money, it is a not-for-profit organization and therefore is not a business.

Sharing the Good News

When sharing the Good News with Muslims, it is good to have tools such as "The 4 Spiritual Laws," "The Bridge Illustration," "Camel Method," "DMM" (Disciple Making Movements), and "T4T" (Training for Trainers). It is useful for us to have these and other tools that assist us in reaching people for Jesus. Yet Jesus did not use tools in proclaiming the Kingdom of God. He could have. Jesus could have taught His disciples "5 Steps to Peace with God." He could have, but

He didn't. Everything He did worked out of relationships. So, tools are helpful, tools are good. Yet, we are not to rely on the tools to tell people about Jesus, rather we are to rely on His love. Jesus' primary strategy for delivering His message was and still is—love.[22]

Ministry is to flow out of our natural way of life. Jesus often did what He did and said what He said to fulfill specific Old Testament prophecies. Nonetheless, He never seemed to be in a hurry.

Nowadays, evangelism is often a planned event. However, most opportunities to witness for Jesus are going to come from natural, normal, daily interactions with people. Consider Jesus' everyday life. From Mark 2, where Jesus calls the disciples and begins what we call His "public ministry," to Mark 15, where He is called before Pilate, the New International Version Bible has fifty-eight subheadings. In exactly fifty of these passages Jesus is teaching and healing—ministering to others. Jesus knew what He was going to do in advance, yet He planned these ministry times to occur naturally in the course of daily life. In other words, they don't appear to the disciples and others to be planned events.

Whether Jesus was walking along a road, or at home, or in the synagogue, people spontaneously came and questioned Him or asked Him to be healed. If you study Jesus' "ministry" opportunities, you will discover that roughly eighty percent of His ministry, or two-thirds of His outreach, happened in the natural flow of His life. There were no planned evangelistic crusades. There was no canvassing door to door. There was certainly no hanging out in a coffee shop, praying for a chance to share. While "ministry" is often something we plan, more often than not, real "ministry" happens in the ebbs and flows of our daily life and work. Ministry is a by-product of our relationship with Him. The ministry done by the disciples and Jesus was not by design, nor by a set strategy. The ministry of Jesus and the disciples happened in the natural course of living out their day. This begs the question: "Do we equip our church members to minister throughout their normal daily activities?" If not, we need to recalibrate.

Jesus prioritized people. Many people cried out for Jesus' attention.

Nearly every chapter of the Gospels talks about the crowds that were always around Him. Yet in the midst of the crowds, Jesus' observations of people are amazing.

He singles out the man with the paralyzed hand.[23]

He notices a woman who touches His garment.[24]

In the midst of a huge crowd He sees a tax-collector sitting in a tree.[25]

From a great number of disabled people sitting by a pool, He singles out the one who has been sitting there for thirty-eight years.[26]

When the disciples rebuke the children, He calls them to Himself.[27]

When the disciples rebuke the Canaanite woman, Jesus blesses and heals her daughter.[28]

When the disciples tell Him to *send the people away*, Jesus says to *feed them*.[29]

There are many more examples of Jesus' discerning observations of individuals throughout the Gospels. Take time to study them for yourself.

Jesus' way with people offers an alternative to our Christian culture's dominant way of relating with others. In our lives, there is an awful lot of *passing by on the other side*[30] that makes up normal relational life today. We simply miss one another, whether it is because we are moving too fast, or we are fixated on our own agendas. Jesus does not want our excuses, and not even our sacrifices. He simply wants mercy, love, prayer and obedience.

The Gospels reveal Jesus as a person who was intimately involved in the lives of the people He encountered. Whether it was the crowds that swarmed Him, the enemies that criticized Him and ultimately killed Him, or the friends and followers who stuck with Him, Jesus was immersed in a network of relationships. Jesus was *with* people.

When we are conversing over a cup of coffee with an acquaintance, discussing plans around a conference table with co-workers, or sitting at the kitchen counter with our teenager, how are we paying attention to others in a manner reflective of Jesus' way? How are we noticing the people in our midst? WWJD?

Time is required to get to know people. When I first went overseas, our mentor, Greg Livingstone, would tell us, "The best way to reach Muslims is to log hours with them." In other words, spend time with the people and build a relationship with them. Being in the marketplace is so strategic because business is all about people. As I considered the best ways to log lots of hours—get time—with people, I came up with three good ideas:

- One, join their military. Then you are with your fellow soldiers day and night. However, this is difficult, as few Muslim armies welcome zealous Christians or Americans.
- Two, follow in Paul's steps and go to jail with people to be a witness to them. My dear friend Moses served in Pakistan for over fourteen years. During that time, he was arrested on false charges and as a result spent thirty-nine days in jail. He told me it was his most fruitful period of witness in all his time working among Pakistanis. Likewise, the Moravians sold themselves into slavery to reach people. Maybe we need to give going to jail to be with people a closer look.
- Three, get a job and work alongside the people. Spending eight or more hours a day working alongside people is a lot of time. As co-workers get to know us and as we shine our light, they will see it. People need to experience His love through us, just like people did when Jesus walked the earth.

Jesus' life touched the lives of others. His head, hands and heart were available to those He lived with. He walked their journey with them, as a friend. He was not distant. He lived in their stories and He invited them to live in His. If logging hours is key to building a relationship, and if working alongside someone is a great way to get time with them, what does God think of the notion of work and witness?

Consider: what needs to be recalibrated in the ways we share the Good News?

Work & Worship

In the New Testament, ministry was not an event that you planned. Likewise, Jesus never called us to do ministry, reserving a few select hours of our day or week for ministry activities. He called us to be with Him, allowing ministry to be a natural outflow of our relationship with Him. The Apostles did not train people to do ministry. They discipled and equipped them. In the Bible, ministry is not a project. Ministry is a relationship—a relationship first and foremost with Jesus. Everything we do—our thoughts, our actions—should reflect God ministering both in us and through us. Ministry is to be a natural outflow of our life.

The Hebrew words *avodah* and *sharath*, plus the Greek words *diakonia, latreias, leitourgias*, though translated in our English bibles as "ministry," mean much more than that. Ministry is not something we plan and then implement; ministry flows out of our relationship with Jesus and impacts everything we do. As we will explore in the next chapter, there is no separation in God's view of work, service and worship.

The Holy Spirit reminded the church in Colossae, *And whatever you do, in word or deed, do everything in the name of the Lord Jesus, giving thanks to God the Father through him.*[31] Worship is to be integrated into every area of our lives and work. My pastor often tells our church, "If you are engaging in an activity—any activity—at work or home or play and it cannot be done in a form of worship, then it should not be done."

Christians have come to associate "worship" almost exclusively with prayer, singing, and sermons with church meetings. When we talk about our churches, we often discuss their worship style. Our religious vocabulary is disconnected from the work we do the rest of the week.

When asked "What is the greatest commandment?" Jesus replied, *"Love the Lord your God with all your heart, and with all your soul, and with all your mind. This is the first and greatest commandment. And a second is like it: Love your neighbor as yourself."*[32]

Throughout history, these two commands have always been listed in that order: Love God, Love others. It is imperative to keep these two commands in their respective order. If you reverse them and love people first, you will discover you cannot sustain your love and you will burn out. In addition, you will likely make an idol of serving others. Only love emanating out of a primary love for God endures forever. That kind of love must flow out of a life of worshipping Jesus.

Summary

What needs to be recalibrated?

We need to recalibrate our perceptions of work and worship, so that they come together. The two need to become one. Work is worship, but church is not work. Let's change our vocabulary and change our actions. Let's call the worship service what God intended it to be—a *Celebration Meeting* or a *Praise Service*, held in the celebration center, led by a celebration pastor and a celebration team. We need to distinguish "church worship" from worship that we do daily in our workplaces and homes.

We need to recalibrate our discipleship. We need to prioritize teaching our marketplace people how to worship at work. We need to give them practical examples—specific ways—of how to live out their faith at work. We need to disciple people in their places of work and in the community, not just at church and in homes.

To summarize succinctly: We need to get to work to worship God, meaning—we need to worship God through our work.

What needs to be recalibrated in the ways you minister the Good News?

4

RECALIBRATING OUR VIEW OF GOD'S VIEW ... OF WORK

Don't count the days, make the days count. —Muhammad Ali

For we are God's handiwork, created in Christ Jesus to do good works, which God prepared in advance for us to do. —Ephesians 2:10

———

CONSIDER THE PHRASE, "It's just business." For a true Christian, it is never *just business*. It never will be. If it ever becomes *just business*, it will mean that business is very bad. The Bible commands us, "*whatever you do, do it all for the glory of God.*"[1]

All theology obviously needs to begin with God's Word and God's works. BAM's theology of work is rooted in the understanding of the Hebrew and Greek languages. There are many examples and words that are misunderstood and arguably mistranslated into English. For starters, consider the Hebrew word עֲבֹדָה (*avodah*). The Hebrew word עֲבֹדָה "*avodah*" (spelled *avodah* or *abodah* or *abodat*) has as its root *avad* or *aved*. *Avodah* is translated in the English Bible from the

Hebrew in three distinct ways according to the context of the verse. They are:

- service – servant/slave
- work
- worship

In the Hebrew language, *avodah* is both a noun AND a verb, and as a verb it remains *avodah* in all verb tenses.

The noun עבדה (*avodah*) occurs one hundred and forty-five[2] times in Scripture. The root verb עבד (*avad*) occurs two hundred and eighty-nine[3] times in the Bible, mostly in the qal form. This does not include the substantive form, עבד (*avad*), which occurs an additional seven hundred and eighty times in the Old Testament. The point is this is not an obscure word. While *avad* is most often translated "service," (Exodus 21:2), or "worship" referring to the worship of YHWH (Joshua 24:14), it is also translated as "work" or "cultivate" or "common labor" (Exodus 5:18). It is of note that this word refers to both "secular" vocations, such as the work performed by the nation of Israel in making bricks while under Egyptian bondage (Exodus 5:18), as well as "sacred" work, such as work within and around the tabernacle (Numbers 3:8).

Avodah is first found in Genesis 2:15: *The Lord God took the man and put him in the Garden of Eden to work it and take care of it.* Here, God tells us that His original design and desire is that our work, our service and our worship—our *avodah*—is to be a seamless way of living.

In other words, laying aside our historical and church perspectives for a Biblical perspective; this means that service, work and worship are one concept in God's mind. **God receives work as worship done unto Him.** Put simply, **work is worship**; or at least it is designed to be in God's eyes. The similarity among these concepts clarifies that God views our actions—our work—as worship; in that it is not done for our own benefit, but rather as an offering to Him. This validates that the workplace *is God's place*. We are to interact with God and talk about God in our workplace just as we do at church or at home. Our place of work is a place of worship where we may express the compassion of Christ in word and deed. Paul affirms this, stating, *And whatever you do, whether in word or deed, do it all in the name of the Lord Jesus, giving thanks to God the Father through him.*[4]

Dave Huber does the best job of concisely and accurately pointing out that the עבד word group is translated from Genesis to Malachi in three ways:

- First, [and most frequently in English] *avodah* is translated as "service," where one submits him or herself to the allegiance of another, whether a slave to a master (Exodus 21:6), a son to his father (Malachi 3:17) or a subject to a king (2 Samuel 16:19). For example, in 1 Kings 12, King Rehoboam is asked by the rebellious northern tribes to lighten the load his father Solomon has placed upon them. In return, they promise to serve [*avad*] him as king.
- Second, this word is translated as "worship," either referring to the worship of YHWH (Joshua 24:14; Ezekiel 20:40) or the worship of idols (Exodus 20:5; Psalm 97:7; Joshua 23:7). When He calls Moses to lead His people out of Egypt, God gives Moses this promise: "When you have brought the people out of Egypt, you will worship [*avad*] God on this mountain" (Exodus 3:12).
- Third, *avad* is also translated as "work." This word is used in reference to vocations both "secular" (Exodus 5:18; Ezekiel 29:18) and "sacred" (Exodus 3:5; Numbers 3:8; Joshua 22:27), both paid (Genesis 29:27) and unpaid (Jeremiah 22:13). In Exodus 34:21, God gives further clarity to the fourth commandment regarding the Sabbath: "Six days you shall labor [*avad*], but on the seventh day you shall rest; even during the plowing season and harvest you must rest."[5]

The Hebrew root word reflects a meaning that integrates the English concepts of work—worship—service. There is no equivalent word or concept in English, so for this reason translators most often choose "service" or "serve" when considering the meaning of the text. The cluster of words derived from the root word *avad* reveal God's view of the integration of worship and work. Consider this: an *oved* is a worker; an *eved* is a slave; *avduh* is slavery. Work involves the idea of serving someone. *Avodah Elohim* is the work of serving or worshipping the true God. In the same way that our bodies must eat to continue to thrive and grow, so serving others is a necessary way for His Spirit within us to thrive and grow.

In the 21st century, Jewish scholar Rabbi Ira F. Stone clarifies this in his blog when he writes:

> The Hebrew word for service, "*avodah*," is the same word we use for both work and worship. This is not an accident. Our tradition teaches that the call to serve another does not fall among the activities of leisure. Meeting the dual obligations to sustain ourselves physically and spiritually through service is thus characterized as worship. Similarly, to worship is not a voluntary act, but rather, the taking of full responsibility for our spiritual survival by providing for the physical survival of our neighbors. "*Avodah*" (worship) in Jewish life cannot be voluntary any more than working to meet our own needs is voluntary. ...The true obligation is not merely to worship in words, but to do the difficult work of service."[6]

In 2009, I was involved in the start-up of a restaurant in the Middle East. That motivated me in my travels to visit restaurants that intrigued me. I made notes, took pictures and went into the kitchens to study the various layouts and use of equipment. I was in Santa Barbara, California, when a friend took me to a trendy restaurant off the main drag. The food was good, the service was great and I loved the décor. I asked the waiter if I could talk to the manager. When the manager came out, I told her a bit of my story about the restaurant we were starting up overseas. I asked if I could visit her kitchen and maybe take some pictures. She was very friendly and showed me all kinds of interesting things.

As we returned to our table for dessert, I asked her, "What's your secret? Your food is great, the service is excellent, this place is awesome."

She smiled and said, "That's easy. I'm Jewish."

I replied, "In other words, *avodah*."

Her jaw dropped to the floor as if I had stolen some ancient Jewish secret and she exclaimed, "How do you know *avodah*!" I told her I was a professor of business and taught business from the Bible.

She slapped my arm in a friendly way and said, "Exactly. Everything we do must be done with quality because everything we do; we do for God."

How incredible that Jewish people continue to understand *avodah* in today's world, just as they did in Jesus' day. Jesus never addressed the sacred and secular divide because such a divide never existed in Jewish thinking. As we will learn in the next chapter, that divide would be initially encouraged by the Greek culture that looked down upon work. Then, during the Dark Ages, the Catholic church sought to separate the marketplace from the church in its bid for power over both government and marketplace leaders. The Jewish people of Jesus' day understood that everything they did in work and in the synagogue was to be done to God's glory, as worship unto God—there was no secular and sacred divide for Jesus and His followers.

Work in the Bible is not presented as non-spiritual. God introduced labor (subduing and ruling over the earth) before worship.[7] Ed Silvoso clarifies:

> God did not do it because labor was superior to worship; rather, he did it because in the garden, labor *was* worship. Furthermore, after sin had contaminated the soil, God pointed to labor as the tool to use when dealing with the curse that had caused the ground to no longer spontaneously yield fruit. At that moment, physical labor—

toiling and the sweat of the brow—became the divinely sanctioned means to extract the now-reluctant fruit.[8]

God gave us two clear reasons for His creating mankind. The first is found in Genesis 1:22, *God blessed them and said, "Be fruitful and increase in number and fill the water in the seas, and let the birds increase on the earth."* The second is in Genesis 2:15, *The LORD God took the man and put him in the Garden of Eden to work* (le-avodah) *it and take care of it.* (Some translations here contextualize the fact that Adam was working the soil, so the translation of the word *avad* becomes "tend" or "cultivate.") Right from day one, Adam and Eve were never assigned to be priests because for them worship meant working. Simply put, in a perfect, sinless world, you and I were created to do two things; be fruitful and multiply our lives and to work.

God is clear: one of His primary purposes in creating us is to *avodah*. How, then, should we interpret Genesis 2:15? Does *avodah* mean *to work*, or *to serve*, or *to worship*? The Biblical answer is 'YES' to all three translations. We were created to work/worship/serve. Clearly, work is good and not evil, as work was given to us before The Fall. Work is not the result of sin; rather work is one of the things God created us to do. And as THE Creator, God models how He is a working God. In Genesis 1, there are multiple times where God describes His work as "good." In fact, it was perfect—a standard that He still upholds and asks of us.[9] Earlier we asked ourselves, "What Would Jesus Do?" Can we say at the end of our workday that our work was good? Consider that thousands of years later, God's work still testifies to His greatness,[10] His creation, His love, His Word; we know God through His work.

God tells us to use the fruits of our labors as worship to Him, as is seen in the Levitical feasts and duties such as Deuteronomy 26:2, where those entering the Promised Land are to offer *"some of the first fruits of all that you produce from the soil of the land."*

Similar to *avodah*, there is another Hebrew word *sharath* that is used to describe this work/service relationship; specifically a relationship with a person of higher rank (even up to the highest rank of God relating to us and us to Him). *Sharath*[11] is another reflection of the limits of the English language in our understanding of God's view of work, worship and service. The word is used ninety-seven times in the Old Testament and is also translated as both "service" and "ministry." Between these two words—*avodah* and *sharath*—there is irrefutable evidence in reflecting God's view of the integration of faith and work. To worship, serve, work and do ministry with God and for God, is all one and the same.

The New Testament & Work

In the New Testament there are three words of interest to us. These words διακονία (diakonia), λατρείας (latreias), and λειτουργίας (leitourgias) are each translated in various English Bibles as either "service" or "ministry" or "worship."

- *Diakonia* is used thirty-seven times in the New Testament, by both Jesus and other writers. It means "waiting at table" or in a broader sense, "service" or "administration." English translators translate *diakonia* as either "serve" or "ministry." Our English word "deacon" comes from *diakonia,* because deacons are supposed to serve others.[12]
- *Latreias* occurs twenty-one times throughout the New Testament, generally by Paul. Paul primarily uses it as a form of "serve." However, several New Testament translations render the word as "worship."[13]
- *Leitourgias* is the concept of helping, serving and ministering. Literally, it means "service offered to God," although it is mostly translated as "ministry," it is also translated as "servant." Jesus does not use the word, yet *leitourgias* is used nine times: four times in Hebrews, three times in Romans and once each in Acts and Philippians.

Throughout the New Testament we see examples of the work/service/ministry/worship relationship. Paul refers to this integrated thinking when he addresses the work of Christian slaves. He writes to the church in Colossians 3:22-24: *Slaves, obey your earthly masters in everything; and do it, not only when their eye is on you and to curry their favor, but with sincerity of heart and reverence for the Lord. Whatever you do, work at it with all your heart, as working for the Lord, not for human masters, since you know that you will receive an inheritance from the Lord as a reward. It is the Lord Christ you are serving.*[14]

In the Old Testament, service, work, ministry and worship are an integrated whole in the eyes of God. Likewise, we cannot separate parts of our lives to involve Jesus in some activities and not in others. As with the Jews, Christians must also commit work as worship to the Lord. Understanding the facets of *diakonia, latreias,* and *leitourgias,* in conjunction with words *avodah* and *sharath,* clarifies that in God's eyes our work is worship—ministry. Our work is an offering to Him, an affirmation of our willingness to serve, regardless of whether in the marketplace, a school, or a church.

Os Hillman contributes similarly, "... of Jesus' 132 public appearances in the New Testament, 122 were in the workplace. Of the 52 parables Jesus told, 45 had a workplace context.[15]"

Eight of the parables that Jesus told are related to farming, sowing and sheep. Six parables are about slaves/servants/employees. Five parables involve the rich and deal with money, a pearl merchant, baking bread, and multiple fishing adventures. Clearly, Jesus the carpenter often intertwined His teachings with the workplace.

Nearly four thousand years ago Moses was telling God's people that God gives us the power to earn a living through our work. In Deuteronomy 8:18, Moses reminds the Israelites and us that God is *Jehovah Jireh—Our Provider.* He clearly states, *remember the Lord your God, for it is He who gives you the ability to produce wealth.* As God's children, we are to do good work because it reflects God's glory and blessing on our lives.

God's vision for our work is to be the provision for our necessities of life. Gene Edwards points out:

"When we pray the Lord's prayer, observed Luther, we ask God to give us this day our daily bread. And He does give us our daily bread. He does it by means of the farmer who planted and harvested the grain, the baker who made the flour into bread, the person who prepared our meal. We might today add the truck drivers who hauled the produce, the factory workers in the food processing plant, the warehouse men, the wholesale distributors, the stock boys, the lady at the checkout counter... and *every other player in the nation's economic system*. All of these are instrumental in enabling you to eat your morning bagel." [16]

Summary

Contemporary Christianity tends to prioritize worship over work, yet God's Word in the original languages teaches that true worship often is work. Work is a form of worship. In Mark 10, Jesus is swarmed by people at a moment when the religious leaders ask Him a question about marriage. In answering their question, He says, *Therefore what God has joined together, let no one separate.* The Hebrews struggled with understanding God's perspective on marriage; however, they did not struggle with God's perspective of *avodah*—integrating service, work, and worship. I wonder what He would say to us in the 21st century about our separation of work and worship?

In understanding the integration of work and worship; what needs to be recalibrated? Clearly, our view of how God views work needs recalibration. And if we understand this, it will change the way we do church, the way we disciple, and the way we share God's message with non-believers.

So, that begs the question, "Why are these Hebrew and Greek words translated as they are?"

That's next.

5

DECIPHERING TRANSLATION

Handle them carefully, for words have more power than atom bombs.
—Pearl Strachan Hurd

> *Our words are seeds that blow all around,*
> *some land in our hearts, some land on the ground.*
> *Be careful what you plant and careful what you say,*
> *you might have to eat what you planted one day.* —Unknown

There are doubtless many different languages in the world, and none is without meaning; but if I do not know the meaning of the language, I shall be a foreigner to the speaker and the speaker a foreigner to me.
—1 Corinthians 14:10-11

———

IN THE BEGINNING *was the Word, and the Word was with God, and the Word was God.*[1]

Words are spoken all day, every day. Some words draw people to attention, other words put people to sleep. Words may be impactful or empty. Jesus notes:

> *For out of the abundance of the heart the mouth speaks. A good man out of the good treasure of his heart brings forth good things, and an evil man out of the evil treasure brings forth evil things. But I say to you that for every idle word men may speak, they will give account of it on the day of judgment. For by your words you will be justified, and by your words you will be condemned.*[2]

The Bible has a lot to say about words. John 1:1 prioritizes the importance of God's words and the value they hold. If God calls Himself the "Word," then words are extremely important. Words bring understanding and action. How words are translated also impacts how we understand what is being communicated. Therefore, the translation of words in the Bible impacts both our relationship with God and our understanding of Biblical concepts which are important to our daily life and work. However, few realize there are words in both Hebrew and Greek whose meanings have changed from what they meant in Jesus' day.

In understanding a foreign language, it is important to understand the impact of culture on language *and* communication. Jesus was Jewish, and most of the Bible was passed down to us via Jewish scribes. Therefore, an awareness of differences between the Hebrew culture and the Greek culture, which has influenced the West, is helpful in discerning the root meaning of Biblical texts.

A fundamental difference in the viewpoint of work occurs between the Greek and Hebrew cultures. In the Hebrew culture, work is honored. A skilled craftsman is among the most prestigious roles in society. It is likely this view is based on their understanding of *avodah*. God's view of work is worship, and any skill needs to be performed in a God-honoring way. One of many times that God refers to *skilled workers* in the Bible we read:

See, I have called by name Bez'alel ... and I have filled him with the Spirit of God, with ability and intelligence, with knowledge and all craftsmanship, to devise artistic designs, to work in gold, silver, and bronze, in cutting stones for setting, and in carving wood, for work in every craft.[3]

Consider the Apostle Paul. He was a Roman citizen,[4] the son of a Pharisee,[5] highly educated,[6] a Pharisee himself.[7] He clearly belonged to the privileged class. The fact that Paul cast his vote[8] to stone Christians—including Stephen—and punished Christians who attended the synagogue,[9] indicates he was also a member of the elite Sanhedrin.[10] So, how is it that Paul knew how to work with leather and make tents? There are two explanations:

First, learning a trade was a duty that the rabbis expected every Jewish boy to learn from his parents. "Gamaliel himself said that learning of any kind, even the advanced study of the law, unaccompanied by a trade, ends in nothing and leads to sin."[11] R. Judah said, "Truly labor honors the laborer," and "that not to teach one's son a trade is like teaching him robbery."[12] In Jesus' day, there was no compensation for rabbinic services, such as judging a case or teaching the Torah to students.[13] Therefore, religious teachers and the rabbis themselves had other occupations to support themselves and their families because serving God was not considered a paid full-time profession. A respected first century scholar, Rabbi Zadok, said, "never use the Torah as a spade for digging."[14] In other words, religious knowledge or preaching abilities should not be used for personal gain, but rather as a complementary talent to other, more valuable and more respected skills.

The Pharisees were primarily a society of scholars and pietists, but nearly every Pharisee was a layman:[15] each one worked a trade to earn a living. This meant that every Pharisee mastered a skill, and Pharisees were known to earn their living by working in various trades and professions.[16] Although Paul was highly educated and of an upper-class background, he was also a Pharisee; therefore, he learned to work with leather (make tents) because self-support was the normal way of life for the religious workers of his day.

Second, after the priests and Levites, those skilled in a trade were among the most respected people in the Jewish community. Throughout the Old Testament we read the specific names of skilled workers and the people who were excellent at their job. Moses, as we know, called upon Bezalel in building the tabernacle. Before Bezalel there was Tubal-Cain[17] who worked with iron and brass, and Huram-abi,[18] who worked as an engraver. There were also skilled musicians, such as Jabul.[19] Solomon, Ezra, Nehemiah and other leaders called upon specific tradesmen too. Oholiab,[20] Bezalel,[21] and Huram[22] served Solomon. Zerubbabel and Joshua,[23] Kadmiel and the sons of Henadad[24] are all linked to Ezra. Nehemiah specifically names no fewer than thirty-six skilled workers who rebuilt both the wall and the city. In Proverbs, Solomon makes over fifteen references to work, among them: *Do you see a man skillful in his work? He will stand before kings; he will not stand before obscure men.*[25] Hebrew culture set forth the premise that God honors those who are skilled in their work and this characteristic of God was, and still is, a foundation stone of Jewish culture. As the Jewish restaurant owner in Santa Barbara validated to me, the Jewish culture still views all work as a service being done unto God.

The Greeks on the other hand had a very different view of work. Consider the heroes of Greek culture—Socrates, Plato, Aristotle— three men who were all philosophers and teachers. Socrates split the world into two parts: the material or physical world and the transcendent or mental, non-physical world. Plato taught that our souls are detached from the material world and our bodies. He separated what God intended to be one in an effort to solve the problem of permanence and change.[26] Aristotle was a philosopher concerned with logic, ethics and aesthetics. To this day, these men are often credited with being the founders of Western philosophy. The Greeks honored "thinkers"—the educated, whereas the Jews honored those with calloused hands. Again, notice, the Greeks esteemed thinking above working. The Greeks categorized and discriminated against people according to whether they were "thinkers" (higher class) or "workers" (lower class). There is no doubt that Greek thinking has shaped Western culture and has, as a result, impacted our current Western view of work.

Hebrew and Greek in Conflict

Translating concepts such as *avodah* and *sharath* into Greek is a challenge. How does one integrate the concept of *work/worship/service* into a culture that exhibits a distinct dichotomy between the physical world and the spiritual world? This creates problems for a translator. Let's look first at some of the words that the very first translators (from Hebrew to Greek) had to choose from.

In Chapter 3, we noted that the Greek words *diakonia*, *leitourgias* and *latreias* originally referred to a form of "service" to anyone and originally were not defined as "ministry" or "religious service." The concepts of "service" and "ministry" continue to evolve throughout time. In today's culture, Dictionary.com renders nine definitions for the word "ministry." The primary definitions focus on church work and working for the government as a minister of state. For words that have more than one definition, a dictionary will prioritize the most common meanings first. The first two definitions given are:

1. *the service, functions, or profession of a minister of religion.*
2. *the body or class of ministers of religion; clergy.*

Dictionary.com renders eleven definitions for the word "service." The first and primary definition is: *an act of helpful activity; help; aid.*

The subsequent ten definitions depict "service" in a variety of ways: military services, restaurant services, government services, public communications, repair services, accommodation services, maintenance services, utility services—all various acts of work. The implications are clear: "ministry" is something one does for the church (or government). Service is a more general word that applies to functions/work/labor/assistance done anywhere, whether at home, at church or at a place of work.

Let us go back now to the beginning of Bible translation. "The translation of the Hebrew Bible into Greek in the 3rd century is regarded as the first major translation ever done in the Western world. The dispersed Jews had forgotten Hebrew, their ancestral language, so they needed the Bible to be translated into Greek in order to read it. This Old Testament translation is known as the *Septuagint*."[27] In the 4th century, the Catholic Saint Jerome was said to have "used this Septuagint as the basis upon which his later, better translations of Scripture were based."[28] It later became the source text for translating the Bible into Latin. In addition, he "coined the term *sense-for-sense* translation, as opposed to *word-for-word* translation. A translator was recognized as the bridge for 'carrying across' values between cultures."[29] Because "it is always inevitable that translators will be affected by their own personal set of values,"[30] even today those who are studying to become pastors are usually encouraged to study the Bible in its original languages in order to get a clearer, unbiased understanding of what God is saying.

Translators impact the translated text. Each translator's own life experiences and education impact their understanding and use of words. "The translator's role is inextricably bound to the socio-cultural position of the translator."[31] "Translators will always instill something personal in their work. The outcome is directly linked to the person who produced it."[32] Many Bible verses reflect these differences, which is why we have so many different English translations. In addition to British and American English differences, different classes of people, theological positions and different life experiences impact a translation.

We have seen that the words עֲבֹדָה (avodah), διακονία (diakonia), Λειτουργίας (leitourgias) and λατρείας (latreias) are translated quite differently, and the way those translations illustrate how different people with different experiences and perspectives on life may influence a translation. Before the 4th century, there is no evidence of these Greek words being translated as "ministry." However, Jerome's translation of the Bible into Latin—completed in 405 AD—features the first changes in the meaning of these words. Remember, the translators at that time were all priests (professional Christians). If a priest or churchman reads the words "service" or "work", he would naturally think it means "ministry," because he worked or served in the church. It then follows that these priests would define and determine the translation to fit with their own lives, backgrounds, values, and work. After all, the readers of their translations were also priests. Jerome and the early translators never dreamed that someday lay people would be allowed to read for themselves, "The Word of God."

For nearly one thousand years the Bible was written on scrolls or parchments and each copy of the Bible during those times was written by hand. Most people were illiterate, which is one reason many churches told the Gospel story via art and even stained glass. Prior to the invention of the printing press in 1436 AD, it was out of the question for lay people to own a Bible. Unfortunately, after Jerome's initial translation, hundreds of years passed before the laity were given access to the Scriptures. Thus, by the time John Wycliffe began working on his English translation in the late 1300s, the changed meanings of these Greek and Hebrew words were well established, altering God's intention of the text. These words continue to be misunderstood to this day.

The word *gay* is a contemporary example of how words and their meaning evolve over time. When Maria in *West Side Story* dances around the factory floor and sings, "I feel pretty and witty and gay!" young people today hear something very different from what audiences understood in 1961. In 1973 I dated a girl named 'Gay,' and that year she began asking people to address her by her middle name, 'Anne.' When asked, "Why the change?" she replied, "People sometimes get the wrong impression when they hear that I am Gay." In the late 1960s the homosexual movement began to identify itself as "gay," and still today we tend to associate the word "gay" with homosexuality.

Our language and its definitions are constantly evolving and thus changing the understanding of words.

Translators Impact Our Thinking

Dr. Lera Boroditsky, an Associate Professor of Cognitive Science at the University of California, San Diego, argues that language shapes the way we think. She points out,

> *If your language and your culture train you to do it, actually, you can do it … language guides our reasoning. Language is fussing even with tiny little perceptual decisions that we make. Language can have really broad effects. … That means language can shape how you're thinking about anything that can be named by a noun. That's a lot of stuff.*[33]

Her research stresses that speakers of different languages think differently. So, it is possible for two people of very different cultures and languages to view the same event and come away with very different perspectives and descriptions of what actually happened.

Robert Alter, a Hebrew scholar who completed an original literary style translation of the Old Testament in English after twenty-two years of work, gives us some insight:

> *The moderns tend to think their task is to 'clarify' everything, whereas the Hebrew writers reveled in ambiguities and sometimes were deliberately obscure, Alter noted. "The moderns imagine that every important Hebrew term has to be translated differently according to context, whereas the Hebrew writers made artful use of repetition of the same terms. The moderns think the Hebrew syntax has to be repackaged as contemporary English, thus repeatedly violating the stylistic integrity of the Hebrew."*[34]

At times, God might intentionally want His words to be ambiguous. His thoughts are not our thoughts. His ways are not our ways.[35]

We try to condense every word down to its most basic meaning. Even if we do that out of a sincere desire to obey God fully, what if obedience to Him is wider and deeper than our human minds and hearts can fathom?

20th Century Patristic Scholar Richard Hanson adds,

> It is a universal tendency in the Christian religion, as in many other religions, to give a theological interpretation to institutions which have developed gradually through a period of time for the sake of practical usefulness, and then read that interpretation back into the earliest periods and infancy of these institutions, attaching them to an age when in fact nobody imagined that they had such a meaning.[36]

If we have changed the meanings of the words as they were spoken by Jesus and written down by His Spirit, have we been adhering to the truth? Revisit *avodah* one more time for a moment: to work/serve/worship is one concept in the mind of God. Our efforts to separate these things is just that: *our* efforts. So may I ask, are we placing Socrates and Western culture before Jesus?

In recalibrating, we recognize that God speaks to us in parables. God shows us His way only as a reflection in a mirror.[37] There is a reason we are only given glimpses of the spiritual world. Paul frequently refers to the Kingdom and the Gospel as a "mystery."[38] There are clearly things God does not want us to understand fully. Our assignment is *to walk by faith, not by sight.*[39] As we grow and learn, we gain a greater understanding of God's word and this induces us to realign our thinking with God's thinking. However, we must avoid boxing in God's word or His will. God is so much bigger than we can think or imagine, so we should never limit Him to one of our boxes. Moreover, and more importantly, we do not want to be like the religious leaders of Jesus' day who believed they had everything all figured out and they were so certain of their thinking that they crucified those who thought differently.

Servants or Slaves?

As we consider translations of the Bible, plus our *avodah* (work/worship/service), we also need to consider the Greek word "slave." Diakonos (διακονον) and its forms, as stated earlier, means "servant," or someone who performs a service or executes a task for someone else. The Greek word *doulos* (δοῦλον) means "slave," but in most English translations the word *doulos* or *doule* is translated "servant" or "bond servant," not slave.

There is a big difference between being a servant and being a slave. A slave owns nothing. A slave must ask direction and permission for all things. First thing each day, a slave must ask, "Master, what should I do today?" A slave realizes that his time, his things, and even his physical body belong to the master. A servant, on the other hand, has choices and rights. Servants can come and go freely and even quit a job, if they so choose. Slaves have nothing but what their master grants.

Even a first-year student of Greek knows the difference between the two Biblical Greek words *doulos* and *diakonos*, yet we continue to change them in our teachings. According to Revelation 22:18-19, this is a perilous thing to do:

> *I warn everyone who hears the words of the prophecy of this scroll: If anyone adds anything to them, God will add to that person the plagues described in this scroll. And if anyone takes words away from this scroll of prophecy, God will take away from that person any share in the tree of life and in the Holy City, which are described in this scroll.*

In explaining these words, I am well aware that God is ruling over me and presiding over my writing. Clearly there were servants and bond-servants in Jesus' day. But there are two distinct words in Greek for slave (*doulos*) and servant (*diakonos*). So is God's intent for us to be slaves or servants? Are we to be in control of our lives or Him? In Matthew 25:23, for example, Jesus says, '*Well done, good and faithful* δοῦλε (doule); *you have been faithful over a little, I will set you over much; enter into the joy of your master.'*[40] There are multiple parables[41] in the Bible that refer to those who serve the King or the Master as "slaves" and not "servants." There is **no compromise** in our Master's Kingdom. Too often we as leaders *have* compromised our words and translation of the Greek. We can justify our compromises, yet is *God* convinced?

In researching this change of the word *doulos* from "slave" to "servant," I found the following written about Josef Tson, a Romanian pastor who was exiled for his faith.

During the years in exile, Josef was taken aback by some of the traits of evangelical Christianity in the USA that were foreign to Christianity as practiced in Eastern Europe. As he studied the historical development of American evangelicalism, he discovered that those contemporary characteristics were the fruit of a series of spiritual paradigm shifts. The first took place in the beginning of the twentieth century, when the nineteenth century emphasis on pursuing holiness shifted to a desire for uplifting, ecstatic experiences.

A second change took place in the 1950s and 1960s, which Josef identifies as a "shift from the call to full surrender, to the call to commitment." He explains the difference this way:

"Christian surrender means that a person lifts his or her hands and says to God, 'Here I am, I surrender, You take over, I belong to You; You dispose of me!' But this is America, the country of the independent people! This is the place of 'nobody should command me! I belong only to myself!' A call to surrender, and even more, to full surrender, simply does not go well with such people. Therefore, the preachers, who wanted 'results', and wanted them in big numbers, felt (and gave in to) the temptation to soften the demand, to reduce the cost, to make the message more palatable. And they hit upon the word 'commitment.' You see, commitment means 'I engage myself to do something for you,' or even lighter, 'I promise to do something for you,' but I remain myself and I may or may not keep my promise. We can speak of weaker or stronger

commitment, but be it as strong as possible, it is still my independent self that engages itself in a tentative promise."

This subtle change paved the way for other shifts in the Christian culture.

Josef Tson goes on to say: "One of them came quietly, almost unobserved, through the new versions of the Bible. Translators did not like the term 'bondslave' to be applied to people. Who wants to be somebody else's slave? Therefore, they replaced it with 'servant.' Again, a reflection and demand of the independent spirit!

In the Greek, 'slave' is doulos, 'servant' is diakonos. In the Greek Bible one never, never diskoneo to God—one never serves God; one only douleo to God—that is, one slaves to God. Jesus makes it clear in Luke 17 that however much you do for God, at the end of the day you say, 'I am an unworthy slave; I only did what is the duty of the slave to do!' But all that is gone now, by the replacement of the word 'slave' with the word 'servant'."[42]

We need to recalibrate. Are we servants of the Lord Most High? Or are we slaves?

Summary

Our language shapes our minds and our minds shape our thinking. Therefore, it follows that our language, our words, influence the way we process ideas. Western cultures and languages have been heavily influenced by Greek thinking. The Greeks viewed work as something that peasants and less-educated people engaged in. The Jewish people, conversely, defined by both their culture and language, were shaped by the Word of God and thus esteemed work.

Cultural differences lead us to mistranslate ideas and words. We need to allow God's spirit within us to shape our thinking. We need to allow God's spirit to formulate our words and ways of communicating. We claim to be Spirit-led, but then we allow our language and our minds to limit our thinking, which in turn influences our actions.

While it is the sinful nature of people to place our own desires ahead of God's, we are commanded to *walk by the Spirit and not the flesh.*[43]

What needs to be recalibrated? Whom do we follow in our lives and work: the ancient philosophers like Socrates and Plato, or our Savior, Jesus?

6

LESSONS ON FARMING

THE PARABLE OF THE TWO FARMERS

One of the most delightful things about farming is the anticipation it brings. — W.E. Johns

I am not reaping the harvest; I scarcely claim to be sowing the seed; I am hardly ploughing the soil but am gathering out the stones. That, too, is missionary work; let it be supported by loving sympathy and fervent prayer.
—Robert Bruce, a Scottish missionary to Iranian Muslims

———

ONE NOVEMBER DAY, *a wealthy landowner hired two tenant farmers and gave them each a field, strictly commanding them to bring forth a good harvest the coming Autumn. Through the frigid winter nothing grew except the tenants' visions of a bountiful harvest in the new season, and by April their zealous souls were sorely vexed to begin.*

The wise tenant tempered his zeal with patience. He planted nothing in April. Yes, all he did was plow. He sowed the seed in May, cultivated and watered through the summer, and harvested in September.

However, the foolish tenant planted straightway in April without

plowing; for sowing seed was second only to harvesting in the joy it brought him. Yes, all he did the whole summer was spread seed on the field and harvest. He had no time for plowing first or for cultivating and watering as the crop grew. He had a banner streaming from his tractor with his personal motto, "Plant early, plant often" on one side, and "Harvest every day" on the other side.

In September, the landowner came and asked the wise farmer, "What has my field produced?"

"35,000 bushels," he replied.

"Well done," said the landowner.

Then he asked the foolish farmer, "What has my field produced?"

"7,000 bushels," he replied.

"Why so perilously few?" queried the landowner.

"I know not," replied the fool. "I harvested every day since April."

"You harvested in April? Then when did you plow and cultivate and water?"

The befuddled fool said, "You only told me to harvest. I had no time to waste on those other things."

Then the landowner said, "A command to harvest is a command to plow, sow, cultivate and water." And he tore the banner from the man's tractor, shredded it and cast it into the wind.[1]

It was an early Spring morning. I was visiting a pastor in central Illinois—corn country. The pastor owned a farm and the land had lain fallow all winter long. I rose early and was enjoying the sunrise coming up over the horizon. My reading that day was in Matthew 13. I began reading and picturing the scene of Jesus teaching the Parable of the Sower to the crowds. As I was meditating on the passage, the hired hand who worked the pastor's land drove up the road on his motorcycle and went into the barn. A few minutes later he came out of the barn driving a big red tractor. He went straight to the corner of a field and began to plow.

I continued reading but had that sense that the Teacher wanted to teach me something. The passage emphasizes the need to "see" and "hear" (verses 14 and 15), so I looked and listened. The only thing I could hear was this farmer driving his tractor slowly up and down the field, making deep cuts into the soil. Occasionally he'd turn up a large rock, but basically, he was turning over the weeds, getting the soil ready for sowing. I continued reading, mulling over the scene of Jesus teaching this parable to a crowd of Hebrew fishermen and farmers.

Again, in verse 18, Jesus says, "*Listen!*" Looking back at verse 14, *You will listen and listen yet never understand, you will look and look and never perceive.* "Lord," I begged, "open my ears to hear, open my eyes to see." And then in a flash, I heard it and I saw it. Not with my physical ears and eyes, but the spiritual ones. Plowing! This man was plowing! *Before you sow, you need to plow!*

Reading the parable literally, yes, Jesus does not mention plowing. But my ears and eyes were opened to what would become a life-changing, relationship-changing, *avodah*-changing revelation. Allow me to share with you what I am confident the Lord was teaching me.

First, consider Jesus' audience—probably fifty percent or more were farmers. Everyone had a garden; this was an agrarian society. The audience understood sowing. A parable about sowing assumed the complete farming process that ultimately yields a harvest. This process begins with plowing.

Second, if Jesus told you to take the Walmart property in your town and turn it into a corn field, what would you do? Once you bought the property, how would you begin the transformation of making/turning Walmart into a corn field? Would you hurry off and buy a sack of corn seed and start throwing seed around the parking lot and throughout the building? Of course! Sowers are sent out to sow— right? At least, that is what many seem to believe about this parable: get out there and sow. Do not worry about the state of the soil; our job is to scatter the seed of the Word of God. It is God's job to bring about the results.

Really?

Doesn't God bring about His results *through* us? Didn't He make us His ambassadors, His lights, His salt? Doesn't He know us by our fruits? Didn't He give us His Spirit to do His work through us?

If we go out and start throwing corn seed on that parking lot, what results will we have? Is that obedience, or foolishness? Have we considered the cost?[2] Are we being good stewards of what God has given us?[3]

The crowd Jesus was speaking to clearly understood this; we must first plow up the parking lot and remove any remnants of the building before we can sow any seed. Before we sow, we first must prepare the soil. Growing a harvest begins with plowing and it is only after plowing that we can finally sow the seed. And remember, we can never get a harvest just by plowing.

Jesus invests more time explaining the meaning of this parable to his disciples than any other parable. Clearly, multiple interpretations could be inferred, so He clarifies. And as He exhorts the Twelve, I want to stop, look and listen, to what He is intending here.[4] Occasionally we may get a harvest without plowing, but will it be a harvest that lasts?[5] The parable is clear, there will be no lasting harvest from hard, stony, or weedy soil/people, unless we first plow. In our understanding of this parable about sowing, a significant factor, which was understood by the people of Jesus' day, has been overlooked—that of plowing.

Plowing in the Messenger's Heart

In plowing the Good News, spreading transformation, God often begins with the messenger. The work God seeks to do is two-fold. He is first and foremost working in us, and secondly, He is working through us. He is working in us to perfect us for His glory. He is working through us to spread His glory. God uses the truth and Good News of His Gospel to transform the soil of our hearts. This is what is happening in the plowing process. As we follow Jesus, we learn and live out the wonderful truths He is showing us: we are being transformed (prepared to bear fruit). Those around us are seeing and experiencing His truths through our life and words: the soil of their hearts is being plowed (transformed and prepared for sowing). Plowing, sowing, bearing fruit, and harvesting are all moments of transformation. While we are usually focused on transforming those around us, God is usually focused on transforming us. It is through our being transformed that those around us will be transformed.

When a follower of Jesus is living and working in a place where the heart-soil around them is hard, stony, or weedy, it is even more important that they plow by their example of personal transformation. These witnesses need a different type of training than most churches and traditional missionary trainings offers. The soil may be ready for God's seed in some places because Jesus' disciples have been plowing, fertilizing and working those soils for centuries. However, when reaching out to those who have little or no understanding of Jesus, the challenges are different, even contrastive. At their best, the Muslim, Hindu, Buddhist and atheist worlds are stony ground; but very likely, they are very hard ground. Learning to plow needs to be brought to the forefront of the messenger's preparation if she ultimately hopes to bring forth a harvest among the hard hearted.

The wonderful thing about doing business in a least-reached community and among non-believers in general is that it thrusts us out into the fields where we are constantly, yet naturally required by our life and actions to plow, sow, cultivate and water. When our co-workers observe our actions, that is plowing. By modeling grace, forgiveness and love, people experience the reality and benefits of the Good News. When we naturally involve Jesus in our daily jobs and routines, people *see* the truth about what we know and believe. These types of plowing, in time, change the mindsets non-believers have about Jesus and the Church. For those reaching out to the hard-hearted peoples of the world, learning to plow needs to become their number one priority. If we desire to see fruit among hard ground, wherever that hard ground may be, we need to disciple people in the strategies of sowing AND we need to disciple people in the methodologies of plowing. We need to recalibrate.

There are four lessons I have been learning about plowing. I will share three here and the fourth one in the next chapter.

Lesson One: BEFORE YOU SOW, YOU MUST PLOW!

Have you ever heard a missionary talk about his work overseas where he talks about the food, the culture, the language, and how he loves the people, but then he says *there's no fruit because the soil is hard?* Hard soil is prevalent in the Muslim, Hindu and Buddhist worlds, but hard soil may be found anywhere. The problem is, if a soil is hard, how is the seed to grow? How will there ever be a harvest? In Matthew 13:4–9, Jesus teaches us a bit about farming. There are three main characters in His story: the sower, the seed, and the soil. The sower represents the evangelist, the messenger—you and me. The seed is the Word of God. The soil clearly represents those who hear the Word of God—non-Christians.

Every story has a main character. Who is the main character of this parable? I believe it is *the soil* because Jesus directs most of His story toward the soil. It is the quality of the soil, its condition when receiving the seed, which is His focus. However, we call this the "Parable of the Sower;" not the Parable of the Soil. This reflects we are focused on the wrong character. This is evident when we consider which of these three characters most churches, Bible schools and mission agencies focus nearly all their time and training on. For example, do we recognize that as believers…

- *We* go to church and hear sermons
- *We* go to Sunday school
- *We* attend seminars
- *We* study the Bible

And then, as we prepare to serve the church or go overseas…

- *We* learn evangelistic strategies
- *We* go to seminary
- *We* learn a business or a job skill
- *We* learn the language
- *We* learn how to contextualize
- *We* study the holy books of the people
- *We* go to more seminars
- *We* learn various evangelism and church planting tools: the 4 Spiritual Laws, Blackaby, our testimony, the Bridge Illustration, DMM (Disciple Making Movements), T4T (Training for Trainers), Camel Method, Storytelling … I could go on.

Notice the focus here. All of these efforts are designed to help the sower—you and me. Each of these learning experiences is designed to draw us closer to God, and help us to fit in better with, understand, and be better understood by the people God has told us to reach. *All these things are good.* All of these are important. The sower needs training. But who is the main character in this parable? THE SOIL. Review again the list above; not one of these things makes an iota of impact on the quality of the soil in preparation for receiving the seed. So, we need to ask the Master, *"Are we neglecting something in our preparation and training to reach people for You?"* Is there something we need to recalibrate?

I began to prayerfully wonder, *Why would a sower, an experienced professional sower, sow seed on hard ground? Rocky ground? And weedy ground? Allowing seed to fall in those places is a waste of seed, which costs money.* An experienced sower would never waste seed. Suddenly it became clear: ***A good sower would never sow on such ground.*** That's the point of the parable!

Does that mean that we abandon working with peoples who are hard? Absolutely not! What we need to learn is the necessity of, and ways of preparing the soil for the seed.

Before we go into the fields to sow,
we must first go into the fields and plow.

I have been researching plowing for several years and I have been learning some things, which I intend to share in the next few chapters. First, however, consider—what are some things we are doing to change people's attitudes about Jesus? Whether in our workplaces or in our neighborhoods, what are we doing that is opening the hearts and minds of people to receive the seed of the Good News? Whether in New York or New Delhi, what are we doing that is moving people toward Jesus? Is God blessing these efforts? If yes, keep at it. If not, we need to start by studying the soil we are working in. We need to understand the kind of soil (people) Jesus has us working among. And as with the Sower in Jesus' parable, we need to ask ourselves, *"What's the difference in these soils?"*

Hard—The first soil is hard. The seed never takes root. Hearts are hard. Jesus says, *"Satan comes and takes away the Word."* Hard soil represents people with shut minds and hearts. Shut due to race, religion, family upbringing, social and cultural values, etcetera. All these create prejudices in people's souls, causing them to be closed. Hard people, prideful people, often fear change. Satan snatches them away from seeing, hearing and understanding the truth.

Rocky—The second soil is shallow and full of rocks. This person, Jesus says, *"has no root in himself."* The Message reads, *"there is no soil of character, and so when the emotions wear off and some difficulty arrives, there is nothing to show for it."* This person expresses joy and excitement in the Lord for a few days, maybe even months, but then falls away.

For example, the missionary excitedly tells the church back home, "Mohammed has come to faith! Praise God!" However, one month later Mohammed is back living his normal Islamic life. He doesn't want to see the missionary anymore. The Word was sown, the Word did touch him. Yet was it an emotional decision? Or did he lack the character to persevere through difficulties? Or maybe Mohammed didn't really count the cost. We have all kinds of excuses for

Mohammed, but have we ever honestly asked ourselves, *"Why are some of the new believers like Mohammed?"* Could it be because the sower (us) planted the seed in rocky ground? Could it be that in our rush to get results, we failed to obediently till the soil first, not giving Mohammed a chance to grow? Yes, I am asking: *Is it our fault that Mohammed's life did not bear fruit for Jesus?*

Thorny—The third soil is full of thorns. These people receive the seed and seem to walk with Jesus for a while: six months, a year or three, even longer. But in time, family, money, safety, or hardship slowly choke them and they bear no fruit.

For example, Abdullah comes to faith! Praise God! Yet after his experience with Mohammed, the missionary wisely delays telling people at home. It is only after four months of meeting with Abdullah does the missionary begin to share with friends and the church back home about Abdullah and the times of Bible study with him. However, after eighteen months of meeting together, Abdullah becomes distracted by money or worries or fears, or maybe he is just too busy. Suddenly, boom! Abdullah is gone. As a result, the missionary stops mentioning Abdullah in his letters, hoping and praying he will repent. Nonetheless, several months later someone asks about Abdullah and the missionary realizes the need to confess what is happening. Again, there are a plethora of excuses. The ground is hard. The Evil One is at work. After all, Abdullah was memorizing verses and having quiet times; this must be an attack of Satan. Yet have we ever asked ourselves, *"Why are some of the new believers like Abdullah?"* Could it be the result of planting seed in ground that was full of thorns? The Message says, *"weeds of worry and illusions about getting more and wanting everything under the sun strangle what was heard."* Could it be that in our rush to get results, we failed to obediently prepare the soil first, not giving Abdullah a chance to grow?

Good—And then there is the good soil. Note that there are a variety of good soils, some bearing a harvest that is thirty-fold, some sixty, and still others one hundred-fold.

Growing a harvest requires, among many things, patience. Last

October I was in Wisconsin. A farmer came up to me at a break in my seminar and said, "I'd like to stay and listen to more, but it's harvest time and I have to go bring in my crops." Just as there is a right time for harvesting, there is a right time for sowing. Neither too early, nor too late. Like the foolish farmer in the opening story, too often we are in such a hurry for results that we fail to properly prepare the soil and so the seed yields a crop that does not last; we sow seed that has little chance of bearing fruit.

> *Before we sow, we first must plow, dig up the rocks,*
> *and pull up all the weeds.*

A person's salvation is ultimately in God's hands, yet we are His sowers: His chosen method for spreading the seed of the Gospel. In addition, clearly the Evil One may sow weeds[6] and/or snatch up the seed before it properly takes root.[7] Consequently, when we sow seed in hard, unplowed soil, are we being wise? We cannot always know when a soil is ready for the seed, but there are indicators.

One key indicator is the urgency of the questions non-believers ask of us. Understand that if we are plowing into people's lives, many people will ask questions about the things we do. Initially their questions are out of curiosity. Nonetheless, when non-believers ask us questions about our faith out of curiosity, we tend to get excited and immediately share our testimony or the basics of the Gospel with them. However, usually this is sowing on rocky or thorny soil.

In working with people, we have learned that the first ten to one hundred times a Muslim friend comments or asks a question about our faith, he is simply curious. He is not seeking truth; he simply thought of something and decided to ask about it. But often we take that innocent question as an invitation to share the Gospel. As a result, rather than move him closer to the cross, we push him away. We need to learn to observe the soil—people's hearts and attitudes. We need to be patient and wait for that urgency—"Please, I gotta know!" An urgency to know about the source of our love, patience, mercy—fruits of the Spirit; indicates that the soil is ready for the seed. (Note: for those reaching out to people in their native country and culture, this process is often faster.) However, recognize that a casual interest in our walk with God usually means the soil is still not ready for the seed.

Another key indicator is the witness of His Spirit within us. When an opportunity comes, ask the Holy Spirit, "What kind of soil is this?" Or "How should I answer?" His Spirit promises to speak through us.[8] Whether He prompts us to speak or to be quiet, obey. Too often we share the Gospel out of our own knowledge or experience and we allow the Holy Spirit to sit on the sidelines. We need to discern His timing for both plowing and sowing.

Jesus, in multiple places, clarifies it is our responsibility to prepare the soil. Two examples. First, with the Samaritan woman at the well,[9] note that Jesus did not go right to the heart of the matter explaining who He was. Likely, the woman would have walked away. Rather, He drew her in; first discussing "living" water and the unveiling of her past. This drew her in and opened her heart to learn more.

Second, Jesus tells us, *"By this everyone will know that you are my disciples, if you love one another."*[10] In Scripture, love is a verb. Love requires action. Our loving actions provide His way for us to plow into people's hearts and minds, turning the soil, changing their attitudes about Jesus and His followers. It is in this turning of the soil that God's love is manifested through us. This plowing is part of His process of preparing the hearts and minds of people to receive the seed of the Good News. As with any farmer wanting to grow a harvest, we need to master the tools for plowing, as well as for sowing and harvesting. Applying God's love in our relationships is plowing. Recognizing when people are paying attention, attracted to God's love, reveals the readiness of the soil to receive God's seed.

Please understand, plowing does not mean you stop sowing. Different fields are tilled and sowed at different times. Plowing is not a replacement for sowing. A bountiful harvest requires both plowing and sowing. Hear me, I am not advocating that we stop sowing seed. There are many times where we may meet a taxi driver or a store clerk—

anyone who we may likely never see a second time. If the opportunity is there, YES! Share the Good News with such acquaintances. But we need to ensure God is the one who is prompting us to share. Jesus on multiple occasions, tells us the words of His Father and speaks not of His own accord.[11] We need to walk in His Spirit, remembering that He promises to speak through us.[12] We need to seek Him for the words to speak, and also seek His timing in speaking His words.

Jesus says, *"I tell you, open your eyes and look at the fields! They are ripe for harvest."* The woman at the well and the people of her town, Sychar, were plowed soil—prepared soil. God, in His way, had prepared them for Jesus' visit. Jesus did not go into the city with His disciples to get food, as He had come to this town having another agenda. They were not "just passing by." It was necessary (ἔδει) for Jesus to go there. Jesus knew there were genuine seekers in Sychar, the seeds had already been sown and now was the time for harvest.

Plowing involves prioritizing our witness through our works before our witness through our words. No farmer plows a field without the intention of someday sowing seed in that field. Yes, sometimes a farmer allows a field to lay fallow for a season, but only for a season. In all relationships there will come a time to verbally share the Gospel in words, but we begin by first sharing the Good News through our deeds.[13] We need to discern, in the Spirit, which fields (soils) need plowing or fertilizing or watering or sowing. We must rely on the Spirit's leading and not assume in the flesh, that every field (person) is ready for harvesting. Consider the United States. Hundreds of thousands of Americans have become hard ground—closed to the Gospel. Could this be due to well-meaning Christians who have been sowing in the flesh? And not in His Spirit?

In tilling the soil there are two primary plows that Jesus and the Apostles use to break up the soil: love and prayer. The Scriptures make it clear that prayer and love open hearts, and that will lead to transformed lives; transformation in both the lives of others, as well as ourselves. We will speak more on this in the next chapter, but for now, remember plowing involves two things—***prayer*** *and* ***love***.

*For as you have heard that it was said, 'Love your neighbor and hate your enemy.' But I tell you, **love** your enemies and **pray** for those who persecute you, that you may be children of your Father in heaven.*[14]

Lesson Two: CONTEXTUALIZATION IS NOT PLOWING

Of the three main characters—the sower, the seed, and the soil—only one character changes. The soil. Thus, the logical understanding is that there are four types of persons who hear the Word of God. At least, that is what I have been taught in the past fifty years. But I believe the times have skewed our interpretation of Jesus' words. Jesus knows His audience is full of farmers who know their trade. Why would a sower, an experienced professional farmer, sow seed on hard ground? Rocky ground? And weedy ground? Some may argue that it just fell out of the farmer's bag in those spots. But again, what farmer would waste seed like that? It is like letting money slide out of a hole in your pocket. Certainly, when you realize what is happening, you stop and pick up the money. Having a hole in your seed bag is the same as throwing money away.

We need to understand ... ***A good sower would never intentionally sow on hard ground.***

I met a farmer in New Hampshire where the soil is very stony. He said the first few years, he had to plow the land numerous times both in the Autumn and in the Spring to get out the stones. He would plow the land, only to have dozens of stones rise to the surface. Then he would go back over the land pulling the stones out of the ground. Sometimes the rocks were so big he had to use a tractor to unearth them.

Every professional will study and know his trade. Jesus' farmer certainly knew the soil well. He has likely studied various sources of water too. And in today's world, farmers observe the composition of their soil to know which chemicals and nutrients need to be added. In addition, a farmer will study the weather and possibly the migration of animals and birds that could also impact his harvest. The farmer may even consider the timing of the market so that the harvest will come when prices are at their highest. Even as we prepare ourselves, part of our preparation for reaching those around us must include training in the ways we may prepare the soil (the people) for God's seed.

When, in training people to sow the seed of the Gospel, we usually place the emphasis on mastering various evangelistic strategies and tools. For those serving overseas there is an emphasis on language learning, and contextualization too. Such training is like the farmer who studies the weather, the community, the market, but has never studied his own soil. To study the soil, to impact lives, we need to interact with the soil. We not only need to prepare ourselves and walk in the Spirit, we also need to plow, remove rocks, irrigate, fertilize—get our hands dirty with the people. We need to plow deeply into the individuals with whom God has us living and working. This requires investing time: living, working, modeling—being Jesus to the people around us. And the result of good plowing is that people see our good works,[15] causing their hearts and minds to be changed, altered, opened and then hungry to receive the seed of the Gospel.

Contextualization is good—it helps people accept that we wish to be part of their culture and community, but contextualization is not love. When I dress like the people, set up my home like theirs, eat their food and speak their language, I fit in. This sounds good. It feels good. It is good. But is it *impactful* on the lives we are striving to win to Jesus? Ultimately, most missionaries who strive to contextualize end up experiencing a version of the following ...

The other day my Muslim friends, Zul and Hamida, had me over for Eid el Fitr, their main holiday which is celebrated at the end of the fasting month of Ramadan. Like our Christmas, it is a time for family and feasting. For two years now, I've striven to be accepted and adopted by Zul's community. So, when he invited me to his home to celebrate the Eid, it was a great honor. I went to great lengths to buy appropriate gifts for the family and to wear their festive clothes. After a time of games and food, my host pulled me aside and in front of his family and relatives, most of whom have become my own good friends, said to me using my local name, "Pak

Panjang, you are one of us. You love our food, and you speak our language well. You honor us by your dress, your gifts; you are truly one of us." Inside I was beaming. I felt so good. *For two years, I studied and struggled to learn the ways of my Muslim neighbors. How I longed to be accepted by them so that they could see Jesus in me and realize that Jesus could be in them too. I was quietly thanking God for those who taught me the importance of contextualization and I was thinking, 'Contextualization works! I am so excited! I am so happy! I am truly seen as one of them!' And then Zul asked to me, "Pak Panjang, are you ready now to become a Muslim?"*

The question came with all earnestness, even love. But it hit me like a ton of bricks, for I realized that Zul, Hamida, all my Muslim friends, saw my learning their ways as an effort to leave my faith, my way of life, and convert to theirs! Had my efforts to contextualize touched their hearts? Had my efforts changed their perspective of Jesus? Not one iota.

Contextualization is good. I have benefitted from some ways it prepared me to understand my Muslim friends and it has opened doors into their homes. However, it has done nothing to prepare their hearts to receive Jesus. Contextualization is good and important for the *sower,* but it has little impact on the *soil.* I believe God's assignment for me is greater than merely being accepted by the people. Rather, as His ambassador my assignment is to bring people to a point of accepting Jesus; that *He* may live among them, not me.

Understand there are two types of contextualization, "worker contextualization" and "Gospel contextualization." Worker contextualization refers to the things a worker does to "fit into" a culture (dress, food, habits, attend mosque, etcetera). Gospel contextualization is sharing the Gospel in their own language and discipling people in the ways they decide (not the foreigner) are culturally acceptable. Allowing new believers to worship God in their own culturally relevant and personable ways, is one way that new believers may plow the ground within their own community.

How may new believers contextualize the Gospel if they know little or nothing about it? In the story of the man possessed by a legion of demons,[16] after he is healed, he begs Jesus to follow Him. But knowing that having a Gentile on this team might not be the best thing, Jesus tells him, *Go home to your own people and tell them how much the Lord has done for you, and how he has had mercy on you.*[17] The man knew little about Jesus but what Jesus had done for him. However, Jesus knew one other thing, this reborn man had encountered God and the man knew it. If we believe when people come to Jesus that they encounter God and receive His Spirit, then His Spirit will teach them truth. And if we believe this then we need to trust His Spirit to show them how to live out the Gospel in their context. As foreigners, their culture is foreign to us. It is brash, if not arrogant for us to teach them what they know better than we do. So how does this work?

Monyel and Atan were the leaders of the first church the Master allowed us to plant in Indonesia. Both men were fishermen. They lived in simple houses made from scrap wood, built out over the ocean. The ocean served as their workplace, toilet and dump. Neither man could read or count past ten. Being neighbors and close friends, they came to faith within days of one another, but were led to Jesus by Atan's father. Atan was the first convert in the village and was the local *bomo* or witch doctor. As they were unable to read, and did not have electricity, we gave each family a cassette player that they could wind by hand. The cassettes contained many of the books of the New Testament recorded in the Indonesian language. Every night the families would gather under a Coleman lantern and listen to the Good News.

After listening to three of the four Gospels twice, they moved on to 1 Corinthians.

On one visit when Noah, my Malaysian partner, and I arrived, Monyel and Atan asked us, "Can you teach us what it means to eat Jesus?" They had heard about it in the Gospels, but now having listened to 1 Corinthians 10 and 11 they asked for clarity. Noah, who also grew up in a poor rural village took the lead.

Noah, "What do you mean?"

Monyel, "Can you explain to us what it means to eat Jesus?"

Atan, "Yes, do the Christians in Malaysia and the USA eat Jesus? Tell us how you do it."

Noah, "Yes, we eat Jesus, but Patrick and I cannot tell you how to do it."

Monyel, a bit agitated, "Why not? We follow Jesus now; shouldn't we do this?"

Noah, "If you want to, yes."

Atan, more agitated, "Of course we want to do this! We love Jesus and want to follow His path."

Monyel, "So tell us what you do in the churches in Malaysia and the USA."

Noah, "I'm sorry, I know how Malaysians and Americans eat Jesus, but I do not know how the Sea Tribe people (their people) eat Jesus."

Atan, clearly upset, urged, "We want to be like you. We want to follow Jesus. We want to be good Christians. Tell us what to do!"

Noah, "Yes, you are good Christians, but you must follow Jesus, not Patrick or me."

Atan, clearly disappointed, "So what do we do?"

Noah, "You listen to the tape and then ask the Holy Spirit what to do."

Noah and I then went to bed. Monyel, Atan and two other men gathered and listened to the 1 Corinthians and Gospel passages several times. They prayed well into the night.

The next morning word went around the village that all the believers were to gather at noon to celebrate the eating of Jesus. At noon we all gathered at Monyel's home. While the men and children sang and prayed, they instructed the women to prepare a meal for everyone. They did this because in the Gospels it says, "while they were eating."

When the meal was ready, everyone sat down to eat. As is their custom, the women and girls sat on one side of the room, the men and the boys sat on the other with the food in the middle. Monyel and Atan sat off to the side. When everyone had eaten, Monyel took a piece of bread and Atan took a jar of red tea, plus an empty jar and set them aside. (They used red tea because there is no wine or even grape juice to be found where they live.)

Then they announced, "We are now going to eat Jesus as the Holy Spirit taught us last night."

First, Monyel took the loaf of bread, held it out for all to see and said, "This is Jesus' body." He told everyone, "We eat Jesus' body as a way to remember Jesus' life and suffering for us." He then prayed a wonderful prayer asking for forgiveness and blessing of all the people there. Next, he tore the bread in half, took a bite and passed the half loaf of bread in his left hand to the women and the half in his right hand to the men. Monyel instructed each person to take a bite and then pass the bread on to another until everyone had a bite. Then he asked one man and one woman to say a prayer.

After everyone had a bite of the bread, Atan took the jar of red tea and held it out for all to see.

Then Atan said, "This is the blood of Jesus." He too prayed a prayer of forgiveness and blessing for the people. He told everyone, "We drink Jesus' blood as a way to remember Jesus' life and suffering for us." Then he poured half the jar of tea into another jar. He then took a sip and passed one jar to the women and one to the men. He instructed them to each take a drink. After everyone had a drink he asked another man and woman to pray. There was much rejoicing and laughing after the last "Amen." They were so happy and proud! But none was happier or prouder than Noah and I, for this was the Sea Tribe's first communion and no human had instructed them in what to do. Instead, they listened to and did as the Holy Spirit instructed them.

That was over thirty years ago and to this day they still celebrate communion the same way. The point again is Biblical contextualization is not a foreigner modeling or teaching the traditions of the faith, rather it is allowing the Holy Spirit to guide people into building obedient practices or even traditions that reflect the God created uniquenesses of the culture. We need to keep our faith in Jesus and not in our evangelistic tools and methodologies. Like the demonized

Gentile, the Holy Spirit can instruct believers as well as, or even better than a missionary can. *But when he, the Spirit of truth, comes, he will **guide you** into all the truth.*[18]

Let me repeat and emphasize, *contextualization is good and necessary wherever you live and work,* but especially when working cross-cultur-ally. Contextualization is of value because when we contextualize our lives, we remove barriers and offenses that people may have against Christians or our Christian Western culture. In sharing the Gospel, we wish to remove all unnecessary barriers that hinder people coming to know Jesus. Learning the peoples' language and culture is extremely important as it shows respect and reflects love. And if we are living abroad, Western dress, Western foods, Western ways of living, and Western methods of socializing—Western culture in general—may be offensive. Living a contextualized life will reduce relational barriers, and this is good. Yet, to this point, I have met dozens of Muslims and Buddhists who have come to Christ, yet not one has told me that they came to faith because their Christian friend dressed liked them, worshipped like them, and enjoyed their food. We need to disciple new believers to rely on God for guidance, not us. Our Western ways may repulse people from learning about Jesus; therefore, contextualiza-tion is a necessary part of learning how to sow, but it is *not plowing.*

Lesson Three: PREPARING THE SOIL

LISTEN! **A good sower works the soil before sowing any seed.**

The best farmers understand preparation. They buy the finest equipment and learn how to repair it. They study the soil, they find sources of water, and they know the nutrients within their ground. The best farmers first prepare themselves. But once the farmer is ready, he then needs to prepare the soil before sowing any seed.

"LISTEN!" Jesus' parable teaches us; ***A good sower works the soil before sowing any seed.***

Think about this. Who makes the soil ready for the seed? The soil itself? No, the sower—guided by the Spirit. Who waters? Who fertilizes? The sower. The Holy Spirit works through the sower to plow, to sow, to water, to fertilize, etcetera. If God has told us to reap a harvest, we need to prayerfully discern and study the fields. Some of us are sent to people who are already ripe for harvest, while others are sent to hard ground. If a farmer expects to reap a harvest from hard, stony, or thorny ground, then preparing the soil is part of the farmer's job. Plowing is one step in the many steps needed to bring forth a harvest. And plowing comes before sowing. It is the sower's assignment to prepare the soil BEFORE planting any seeds. Now I know a few people are thinking, well, it is God's job to prepare the soil. Technically it is God's job to convert the lost too. So why bother witnessing? Paul reminds us of God's process when he writes, *I planted the seed, Apollos watered it, but God has been making it grow.*[19]

God gives the growth; we do the preparation. God manages the seed. It is our responsibility to tend the soil. Yours and mine, not the angels'. God grows the seed through us and with us. God uses us to prepare the soil. This is the assignment of every sower. If we are going to see a harvest we need to plow before we sow.

Some may be thinking, well what about the three verses where Jesus talks about the fields that are ready for harvest? Read the text. In Matthew 9[20], Jesus had been plowing, watering, fertilizing—working the soil for at least a year in advance of these teachings. Yet did everyone in these fields respond to Jesus' invitation? Clearly the religious leaders did not. We need to understand that some fields are fertile soil—ripe for harvest, ready for the seed from the first day. Clearly, Jonah did little to prepare the hearts and minds of the Ninevites.[21] This is where our evangelism trainings need to teach both discernment and how to understand the components of various soils.

Jesus is an expert farmer. He has prepared Himself and He has prepared the ground. The seed has been dropped so the harvest is near. The 21st century is our moment. It is our turn to walk in our Master's footsteps. However, if we have only prepared ourselves and not the soil, we can plant thousands of seeds, but they are not going to grow and bear fruit that will last.

Read "The Parable of the Sower" in Matthew 13. The context of this parable in both Matthew and Mark is the people—the people who are blind and deaf to who Jesus is. Many of Jesus' disciples, both then and now, are blind to who Jesus is. Realize that we have only a few snapshots of Jesus' life. As a result, we often build our strategies around what we know of ourselves, rather than of Him—His Spirit, and the people He has called us to.

This is why we see Jesus investing so much time with the twelve and the seventy. He is daily plowing into their hearts and minds.

Summary

Before we go into the fields to sow, we must first go into the fields and plow. A good sower works the soil before sowing any seed. Are you working on hard ground? Many knowingly sow seed on hard ground, and then blame Satan for a lack of results. Satan certainly causes problems for us and often is the reason behind why the ground is hard. Yet we need to wake up to the fact that hard ground requires deep plowing and that requires effort—hard work on our part.

I remember watching construction workers dig up the cement walkway in front of our home in Hong Kong. First, they worked on the cement with noisy jack hammers, which took nearly a week. Then with picks and shovels they tore up the ground, removing the rubble. It was very hard work. It took weeks to replace that sidewalk.

What needs to be recalibrated?—Training. Preparing the sower to sow is very important, but a well-trained, well-equipped sower is no match for unprepared soil. Let's dig in.

7

THE TWO PLOWS

Farming looks mighty easy when your plow is a pencil and you're a thousand miles from the corn field. —Dwight D. Eisenhower

When you put your hand to the plow, you can't let go till you get to the end of the row.—Alice Paul

No one who puts his hand to the plow and looks back is fit for the kingdom of God. —Jesus

———

GOD HAS CALLED many of us to sow and yield a harvest in hard ground. So, what is Jesus teaching us about yielding a one-hundred-fold crop from hard ground? He's teaching us that before sowing any seed, the hard ground needs to be broken up and made ready to receive the seed. This requires plowing. In spiritual terms there are two primary plows God has given us to break up hard, rocky, and thorny ground. The first plow is *prayer*, and the second plow is *love*.

We need to plow in *prayer* and plow in *love*—love and prayer that are full of His Holy Spirit. These two plows are essential. Like a double-edged sword held in our hands and strengthened by His Spirit, these plows penetrate the soul and spirit, the joints and marrow, transforming the thoughts and attitudes of a person's heart.[1] One plow is not enough. Both plows are essential for breaking up hard ground, overturning rocks and uprooting thorns and weeds. God gives us two plows: the first plow opens up the ground, while the second plow turns over the soil. The ground, or hearts of people, need to be opened. This is the first plow. Then the opened ground or uppermost soil needs to be turned over to bring fresh nutrients to the surface which good seed will then feed on. In addition, turning the soil over buries the weeds so they decay and die.

Lesson Four: THE TWO PLOWS

Plow #1: PRAYER

Many of Jesus' teachings clarify the need for prayer, and none is clearer than Mark 9.

In Mark 9:16-29, some people are arguing with the disciples and Jesus asks, "*What are you arguing with them about?*" Jesus is told there is a boy with an evil spirit whom the disciples cannot cast out. How does Jesus respond? "*You unbelieving generation … How long shall I put up with you? Bring the boy to me.*" The father explains how the evil spirit threw the boy into the fire or water to kill him.

The father then pleads, "*If you can do anything, take pity on us and help us.*"

"*If you can'?*" Jesus responds. "*Everything is possible for one who believes.*"

Immediately the boy's father exclaimed, "*I do believe; help me overcome my unbelief!*"

Here is a man who is likely rocky or thorny ground. His interest reflects he is not hard soil, yet Jesus' response tells us he needs some plowing, some watering, some fertilization, some care. We know this because of the man's lack of faith. He has clearly heard of Jesus' power and possibly even seen Him perform other miracles. Yet when this man approaches Jesus' disciples, he is met with evidence of the disciples' lack of faith. His faith remains weak because their faith is weak—both are still thorny soil. In my own experience, usually, unbelief is strong in the presence of a demon.

So, what does Jesus' plowing look like? It begins with FAITH. BELIEF. *Everything is possible for the one who believes.* And how is faith applied?

"When Jesus saw that a crowd was running to the scene, he rebuked the impure spirit. You deaf and mute spirit," He said, *"I command you, come out of him and never enter him again."* Jesus healed the boy.

Later that day, after Jesus had gone indoors, His disciples asked Him privately, *"Why couldn't we drive it out?"*

He replied, ***"This kind can come out only by prayer."***[2]

Jesus is also plowing into the lives of His disciples and the crowd, and He is plowing deep. In doing so, He is emphasizing the plow of prayer. Yet just being around Jesus is not enough; nor is it enough to believe in Christ's power and desire to be saved. What *is* required is a life of prayer: listening to God's will and believing that He will act. True faith is not only the belief that Jesus is the Christ, but also that He rewards those who earnestly pursue Him.[3] Jesus is plowing into His own disciples because of their lack of faith. If you want to see God work, pray!

We understand that *faith is confidence in what we hope for and assurance about what we do not see.*[4] *And without faith it is impossible to please God.*[5] You only really believe that which activates you. *"I command you, come out of him and never enter him again."*[6] Then is faith one of the plows God uses to break up hard ground? No. Faith is a precursor. Faith is prayer applied. Prayer is needed to build faith and is essential to having an intimate relationship with God. The first plow that we need to use if we are going to break up the hard ground is prayer. We must remind one another of the need to pray and not quit.[7]

This prayer is not simply a 'God bless you' type of prayer. It is an intercessory prayer; a joining with God in asking His will to be done, first *in* our own lives and then *through* our lives. It is a prayer that heals the hurting—physically, emotionally, and spiritually. It is a prayer that binds up Satan's work here on earth. It is a prayer that never ceases. It is a prayer that transforms our own lives, empowering His presence within us to transform the lives of others through simple obedience. Prayer is the conduit for His grace and love to flow into our lives so that it can flow through us, drawing the lives of others to Jesus.

The key to opening hearts is in the hand of Jesus, and that key is PRAYER. Intercessory prayer requires a close relationship with Jesus. All prayer infers communion with the King of Kings. The key to reaching the lost is *not* found in strategies, methodologies, education, or even evangelization tools. The key is PRAYER, as in *pray therefore to the Lord of the harvest.*[8]

To many people, prayer does not seem practical; it is absurd. We must realize that prayer seems like foolishness from the ordinary, common-sense point of view.[9] Too often we are taken up with tasks—active work—while what we need is prayer to break up the hard soil. We waste our Lord's time in over-energized activities when what we need is prayer. Understand, we are called to belong to Jesus. We are not above our Master: we are not to dictate to Jesus what He needs to do. It is important to remember that our Lord calls us first and foremost to Himself, rather than to any special work. And prayer will lead us to a life with Jesus.

The first plow needed to break up hard ground is PRAYER.

Plow #2: LOVE

Throughout the New Testament we find there is a second plow necessary for breaking up hard ground.

Consider, when Jesus is asked, *"Teacher, which is the greatest commandment in the Law?"*

He replied, *"'Love the Lord your God with all your heart and with all your soul and with all your mind.' This is the first and greatest command-*

ment. And the second is like it: 'Love your neighbor as yourself.' All the Law and the Prophets hang on these two commandments. "[10]

The absolute greatest commandment—and even the second greatest—is to love: love God and love others. To love God is the greatest thing we can do in life, and the second greatest thing is to love our neighbor as ourself. The Law and the Prophets hang on LOVE.

Jesus also tells us that people will know we are His followers by our LOVE: *"A new command I give you: Love one another. As I have loved you, so you must love one another. By this everyone will know that you are my disciples, if you love one another."* [11] So how do we love someone else? John, the disciple Jesus loved, urges us: *"Dear children, let us not love with words or speech but with actions and in truth."* [12] The Living Bible clarifies: *"Little children, let us stop just saying we love people; let us really love them, and show it by our actions."* Love is an action and not simply words. While feeling love and saying "I love you" are good and nice, true love involves actions and not simply words. For example, a suitor may tell his beloved he loves her a thousand times a day, but if his actions don't reflect that, will she believe him?

In Luke 7, John the Baptist sends two disciples to ask Jesus, *"Are you the Messiah or should we look for another?"* [13] Jesus does not reply with observations of His great knowledge of Scripture; nor does He remind John's disciples of the dove descending on Him at his baptism. Rather Jesus says, *"Go back and report to John what you have seen and heard: The blind receive sight, the lame walk, those who have leprosy are cleansed, the deaf hear, the dead are raised ... "* [14] Jesus is directing them to tell John "what you have seen and heard Me **DO**". The Gospel is not merely written or spoken *words*, yet so much of what we are taught about sowing the Gospel has to do with preaching or proclaiming. Preaching and proclaiming is one part of God's strategy for winning people, yet love is His supreme strategy. Love is central to a God-like witness for Christ and love requires action. Seeing is believing. People are more likely to believe what they see and less likely to believe what they are told. People are more likely to trust our actions—which usually reflect our intent—than they are our unproven words. James agreed when he wrote, *"In the same way, faith by itself, if it is not accompanied by action, is dead. But someone will say, 'You have faith; I have deeds.' Show me your faith without deeds, and I will show you my faith by my deeds."*[15]

A younger overseas field worker wrote to me: *This past week I was doing a quarterly review with one of our designers and one of the things he said to me was, "Boss, you need to be more mean to me, even if it's just a little bit." I asked him, "What do you mean?" He went on to explain that there are no other bosses in Pakistan who treat employees the way I do. "You're too nice!" he exclaimed. He's worried that if he ever stopped working for me, he wouldn't be ready to work under an obstinate boss. This led us into an hour-long conversation on why, because of what God has done in me, I could never be a 'mean' boss, and how God Himself is a loving, kind and compassionate God who isn't out to get you, or use you, but rather looking for a personal relationship with you.*[16]

Words are important and have impact, but actions that back up our words are powerful. Paul wrote, *For the kingdom of God is not a matter of talk but of power,*[17] and *because our gospel came to you not simply with words but also with power, with the Holy Spirit and deep conviction. You know how we lived among you for your sake."*[18] Jesus taught us that our love is the key to winning people to Him. In 1 Corinthians 13 we learn about love.

Love is patient, love is kind. It does not envy, it does not boast, it is not proud. It does not dishonor others, it is not self-seeking, it is not easily angered, it keeps no record of wrongs. Love does not delight in evil but rejoices with the truth. It always protects, always trusts, always hopes, always perseveres.[19]

When we are patient, kind, protecting, persevering—applying love in our daily lives and work, the people around us recognize we are different. Paul lived and worked among people while demonstrating God's love and this softened their hearts and prepared them to receive with eagerness the message of the Gospel.

We want to see lives transformed by the power of the Gospel. But a transformed life requires a transformed heart. Or, as Jesus puts it, *"you must be born again."*[18] The heart is reborn through experiencing God's love and understanding Jesus is the personification of that love. Experience and understanding allow a person to choose to surrender themselves to Jesus so that He may rebirth them. Experiencing God's love comes from seeing and interacting with us—those who personify the love of Jesus. Understanding comes as we verbally explain to them about Jesus, and they seek to know more. Experiencing and understanding His love usually takes time.

Be patient as you speak the truth of the Gospel and tell the story of Jesus. Be patient as you share your testimony. Be patient as you model faith, love, grace, and forgiveness in Jesus' name to those you live and work with. Don't rush as you thoroughly plow the Good News into people's lives and model the love of Jesus. Ears will open as they hear Jesus' words through you. Hearts will open as they see Jesus' life through you. In other words, speak the truth into people's lives and live out your faith. With an open-heart people can hear God's words. Few people are argued or talked into the Kingdom. When people *see* the Gospel, they will then *listen* to the Gospel.

The following anecdote is a simple illustration of our increased ability to trust and believe based on *seeing is believing*. I fly through the Detroit airport frequently where, inside the terminal, there are several huge televisions. When the shopping network (QVC) is on, there is often a guy with a beard selling products and one of his favorites seems to be a set of kitchen knives. I have watched him many times take one of the knives and cut through a bunch of carrots with little or no effort. Each time I watched him, I thought to myself, "Yeah, right. A knife is going to float through a bunch of carrots that easily. The demonstration must be rigged." Shortly after one such episode I was visiting a friend in Louisiana. I offered to help his wife prepare dinner, as he was changing clothes. She handed me a knife and a bunch of carrots and asked me to chop them up. I took the knife and came down hard on the carrots. The knife went through the carrots like they were soft butter. Surprised, I exclaimed, "Wow! Where'd you get this knife?!" She responded, "Oh, I got them from the QVC shopping network. You know, the ones the guy with the beard sells." Guess what I did the next time I saw that ad in the Detroit airport? I wrote down the number to buy the knife. Seeing is believing.

Paul considered the Bereans to be more noble in character than the other Jews in Greece because they studied and examined the Scriptures every day to see if what he said was true.[20] I encourage you to study the life of Jesus. In Jesus' ministry, He rarely spoke about the Kingdom of God without first demonstrating His authority by performing a miracle or an act of love.

The second plow needed to break up hard ground is LOVE.

Seeing is Believing

People from different cultures, backgrounds, or races may use words differently. This often leads to a misunderstanding of Biblical concepts. Actions speak louder than words. If we are going to use this plow of Love, we need to be in ongoing relationships with people. Personal interaction creates opportunities for God's love to reach through the many layers of a person's mind and heart. A person needs to see love and experience love, to understand it. People can *see* His love in His care for us and in our care for others around us. They can *experience* His love when we care for them and those they love. They can *understand* His love when we get our own culture's definitions of love out of the way and allow Jesus to use our Christ-like actions to reveal His love in their context. We often assume that their view of forgiveness, grace and love is the same as ours, but often it is not. This is why actions— Jesus-like, loving, sacrificial actions—are much more important than words. As we commonly say, *Seeing IS believing*.

Remember Sue, my office manager from chapter 2? Multiple times over the first three years, after seeing me apply grace or forgiveness to a person's work she would remark to me, "Oh that's what you mean by grace." Or, "Your perspective on forgiveness is different than ours; I never thought of forgiveness like that before." Seeing IS believing.

We have to make the Gospel incarnate—give it substance—before we proclaim it. We must lead by biblical example and model God's goodness in our everyday lives. Dr. Herbert Kane taught this poem to his students when he was teaching at Trinity Evangelical Divinity School:

> *You are writing the Gospel a chapter each day,*
> *By the things that you do and the words that you say.*
> *People read what you write whether distorted or true,*
> *What is the Gospel according to you?*[21]

In other words, humility is an important component in modeling the Gospel. Drew, who owns a business in a fundamentalist Muslim country, writes,

> *Last week I was downtown getting some documents for my visa application. I parked on a street that I park on every time I come, in a spot on the roadside in the middle of a long line of parked cars. After I got what I needed, I came back to find an angry shopkeeper telling me I wasn't allowed to park in front of his store. I could tell he was wanting to get into an argument and a crowd was gathering to watch what they hoped would be a fight, so I calmly told him that there was no sign, that no one had told me, and that the entire street had cars parked along it. As I drove off, I realized that he had emptied the air in my tire and I was driving on my rim. I had to get out in the middle of rush hour, in the heat, and change my tire. As you can imagine, I was a little frustrated and upset at the store owner. As I drove back to the office however, I had to stop myself and check my emotions. God has taught me the past couple of years that I need to be very aware of what emotions I'm having, as my emotions are a barometer for my heart. I needed to repent and get my heart right. I also felt God was telling me I needed to not just forgive the guy but go farther and bless him. It felt kind of awkward, but I decided that I'd buy him a traffic cone to put in front of his store. Wanting to communicate clearly that even though he had done me wrong, God wanted me to do him good and bless him, I shared this plan*

with an employee and asked him to help me. When my employee heard what had happened and what I felt I needed to do, he was amazed. He told me, "Drew, our religion teaches many things about forgiving people and doing good to others, but when I sit at home and talk with my family, I tell them that we teach doing good, but only you Christians do good." I was able to share with my employee how I am able to give grace because of the grace God has given me. It's when we truly understand God's grace that we can forgive and even love those who hate us. The next day when we visited the shopkeeper to give him the traffic cone, he was the one excitedly explaining to the shopkeeper and the people who gathered (they thought I might be back to have the fight we didn't have the day before once I discovered the flat tire) that we want to bless instead of fight, and that though this isn't the normal way to do things that maybe this is the way it should be.[22]

Another evangelist told me the story of how he had been turned over to the police by his neighbors for violating the anti-conversion laws. After he was released from prison, he devised a plan to start a small business which would help the families who had betrayed him. In this way, he was able to spend time mentoring the youth in his community. The same elders who had asked the police to arrest him later came to ask why he continued to show them forgiveness. He responded, "God sent me here to be a blessing to you all and demonstrate His love. You can kill me if you like, but I must obey what He tells me to do." His persecutors now attend a fellowship that he leads. Speaking the Good News is wonderful! Living out the Good News in our actions is powerful!

Quality Plowing Requires Time

I have several farmer friends who have validated that plowing is harder work than harvesting. To plow up a hard field takes time. To plow up a hard heart takes time *and* effort. In the book *Outliers*, author Malcolm Gladwell researched and discovered that it takes roughly ten thousand hours of practice to achieve mastery in a field. Master a language? Ten thousand hours. Master a job skill? Ten thousand hours. Master a relationship? Ten thousand hours. Gladwell's research proves that time is an essential ingredient in the success of any venture. Invest ten thousand hours in any skill and you will likely become an expert. Paul relates to this in 1 Corinthians 3 when he refers to himself as a "master" or wise builder. He has invested the needed time to impact lives for Jesus.

Nine years ago, a mission organization working in Muslim areas did a survey to learn how many hours a week their members were spending with Muslims. The survey concluded that on average their field workers or "missionaries" averaged three to five hours per week with Muslims, and that time might be divided between more than one Muslim friend. To keep things simple, let's assume we're considering one Muslim friend per year, at five hours per week. That's two hundred-sixty hours per year. Now if we allow four weeks for vacation, it will take over forty-one years to achieve ten thousand hours with *one* Muslim friend. While God can break through and work a miracle in any person's life and heart at any time, in my thirty-seven years of living overseas, I have witnessed only four times a Muslim turning his life over to Jesus as a result of such a miracle.

Now compare the traditional missionary approach which yields five hours a week with a business or workplace approach. In the workplace we usually work alongside local people six hours a day or more, five days a week. If we calculate that out for forty-eight weeks a year, it will take just under seven years of plowing to reach ten thousand hours and thus a greater possibility of a breakthrough. So, in order to get ten thousand hours with people (whether at home or overseas)—to find the amount of time necessary for such plowing—we get a job and we work alongside the people we are called to reach. We can also start businesses and create jobs for them, thus giving us the opportunity both to model and tell them the truth of the Good News. *This* is *plowing*. This is sowing into people's lives. This is becoming a Paul-like master builder.[23]

Plowing and sowing the Gospel into people's lives requires time. The majority of B4T businesses I have worked with do see fruit in the shape of baptized believers—and interestingly, this usually occurs between years six and eight. That said, the ten-thousand-hour rule is not a hard and fast rule. It is a guideline. It is something I've observed, something intended to be an encouragement: a goal in building relationships. Nowhere in the Scriptures does it say that we will magically see fruit in seven years or ten thousand hours. Ten thousand hours is simply a benchmark to encourage us to persevere, to stay on God's farm, to keep moving forward, to plow.

I confess, for years I knowingly sowed seed on hard ground, praying and hoping for God to bring a harvest. And for decades I blamed Satan for the lack of results. And though Satan is certainly a part of the problem, the real problem was me. I did not understand that hard ground requires deep plowing—pouring myself into the lives of those without Jesus, that they may experience His love and grace for themselves through me.

Understanding this, our priority should lie in finding large blocks of time with those we are trying to reach. The objective of investing more time with people is to increase the likelihood that they will both see and hear the Gospel in and through our lives. We can do this with **work**, but not just by the duties we perform with our physical bodies. If we allow Jesus' Spirit to work through us, our work becomes WORKSHIP or *avodah*—the integration of faith and work.

Paul tells the church at Corinth, *"My message and my preaching were not with wise and persuasive words, but with a demonstration of the Spirit's power, so that your faith might not rest on human wisdom, but on God's power."*[24] Our work is not about methodologies or tools; it's about demonstrating God's power. The ten-thousand-hour rule is simply an encouragement to press on. Strategies, tools and guidelines are all helpful, but in recalibrating missions, such ideas and methodologies can be dangerous. They tempt us to rely on our own work, our own thoughts, and our own ideas, instead of on Jesus'. We need to recalibrate around the most powerful tool God has given us as His witnesses—sacrificial, Holy Spirit-empowered **LOVE**.[25]

Preaching & Proclaiming

If you pause and think about this Parable of the Sower, our commonly accepted interpretation of the parable seems illogical. The way Jesus explains all His other parables we can readily agree, "Yes that's exactly how it would happen in real life." But the Parable of the Sower deviates from that pattern—it does not make sense that someone who grows crops for a living would intentionally toss seed on a path.

Due to this apparent confusion, it is likely why this is one of the few parables that Jesus explains to His disciples. Many interpret Jesus' explanation as He's saying something like, "Look, you're going to share the word with people, but only some of them will truly take root and multiply. In fact, a lot of people will respond positively at first that won't actually stick with it." However, reread and look closely at Jesus' explanation and consider this teaching not as a stand-alone parable, but in the context of all His other teachings.

> *"Listen then to what the parable of the sower means: When anyone hears the message about the kingdom and does not understand it, the evil one comes and snatches away what was sown in their heart. This is the seed sown along the path. The seed falling on rocky ground refers to someone who hears the word and at once receives it with joy. But since they have no root, they last only a short time. When trouble or persecution comes because of the word, they quickly fall away. The seed falling among the thorns refers to someone who hears the word, but the worries of this life and the deceitfulness of wealth choke the word, making it unfruitful. But the seed falling on good soil refers to someone who hears the word and understands it. This is the one who produces a crop, yielding a hundred, sixty or thirty times what was sown."[26]*

People respond differently when presented with the Gospel.

Initially, and this is especially true overseas; a lot of people will respond positively at first who won't actually stick with it." And that is the way we like to read this parable, possibly so we can feel good about our own failures or have an excuse for our own sins, disobedience or ineptitude in doing evangelism. However, in the context of Scripture, Jesus is not giving us a rationalization for why we do not always get a harvest when we sow seeds.

Note, on hard soil Satan snatches the seed, on rocky soil the seed dies for a lack of roots or depth/maturity/endurance, and on thorny soil the seed dies due to the temptations of the world or distractions or prioritizing self over God. Jesus is explaining this is what happens when we sow on these soils. Yet the one "who produces a crop" is the one who sows on "good soil" (also see Mark 4:8 and Luke 8:8). The implication then is that a good sower, a professional sower, would never waste seed on the other three soils, as only the last soil is "good." After all, who would sow good seed on bad soil?

For example, let's pretend you work for me. I hand you a bag of seeds and say, do the best you can to grow these into a crop and then bring me the harvest. You decide to tear open the corner of the bag and let the seeds fall out where they will as you stroll around the barns, the lane, the yard and the field. Then over the following weeks, when you notice a little plant sprouting that might have been one of your seeds, you clear a little space and water it to see what will grow. At the end of the growing season, you wander around looking for any crop that may have survived. How do you think I, as your boss, am going to respond to the paltry harvest you bring me? "You fool! That's terrible!" And I'd be right to respond that way. In Matthew 25, Jesus describes a master's response to a servant who did not put his entrusted money to good work. *"You wicked, lazy servant!"* And the master throws the servant out. Will our heavenly Master be angry at us for carelessly handling the seeds He has entrusted to us?[27]

The Parable of the Sower clearly accentuates the good soil. Throughout Scripture we know that God is good and His actions are good. Therefore "good" soil is going to be God's soil. In His explana-

tion to the disciples, Jesus is clarifying what is good or God-like soil—
the soft, rock-less, weedless soil.

In stating His mission in the world, Jesus says:

The Spirit of the Lord is on me, because he has anointed me to proclaim good news to the poor. He has sent me to proclaim freedom for the prisoners and recovery of sight for the blind, to set the oppressed free, to proclaim the year of the Lord's favor.[28]

Some read this metaphorically, but Jesus actually freed prisoners of sin and disease. He plainly gave sight to the blind. He literally freed the oppressed.

From studying Jesus' life, we know He always performed some sort of miracle or gave some awe-inspiring insight when proclaiming the Kingdom of God.[29] He validated His authority by demonstrating the power of God within Him. He amazed people both with His words[30] and His actions.[31] In His proclaiming of the Kingdom of God, Jesus utilized both the authority AND the power of God. I believe it's safe to say the Apostles did the same thing in their own ministries. Paul writes to the Romans that one reason he longs to visit them is to impart "some spiritual gift."[32] Multiple times in Acts it is first through the demonstration of the power of the Holy Spirit, then through their words that Jesus' disciples draw people into the Kingdom.[33]

For the disciples, preaching and proclaiming included demonstrating His power and performing miracles. But in today's preaching and proclaiming, do we include these things? Through such acts, Jesus opens people's hearts and minds first—that's plowing, preparing the soil—then He sows the seed. Yes, not everyone receives the seed every time Jesus sows, yet every time Jesus sows seed there are people who do respond, meaning His focus is on the soils who are ready for the seed. From this we may assume that other soils will take more plowing, fertilizing and watering. Preparing the soil is our assignment, not God's. Before we head into the world to sow God's seed, we need to give greater attention to plowing before sowing.

Summary

What needs to be recalibrated? We need to train people to plow. We can overturn the ground and make hard, rocky, thorny soil ready for the seed of God's Gospel by intertwining constant prayer with love that is demonstrated in our daily lives. No soil is a match for a loving prayerful plow.

1 Corinthians 2:1-5 states:

People will know we are followers of Jesus by our love not by the eloquence of our words. When I came to you, I did not come with eloquence or human wisdom as I proclaimed to you the testimony about God. For I resolved to know nothing while I was with you except Jesus Christ and him crucified. I came to you in weakness with great fear and trembling. My message and my preaching were not with wise and persuasive words, but with a demonstration of the Spirit's power, so that your faith might not rest on human wisdom, but on God's power.

The overall message here is that works, not words, change hearts. Yes, words are needed, but consider: is hearing believing or is seeing believing? In training people to witness, we need to emphasize sharing through our actions, as much as, or even more than, sharing through our words. In recalibrating we need to remember that the eyes are the key to opening hearts.

8

MORE ON PLOWING

Truth may be vital but without love it is unbearable. — Pope Francis[1]

With all thy getting get understanding. —King Solomon[2]

———

GOD HAS COMMANDED us to go to the ends of the earth to reach all peoples, but many peoples have hard hearts toward Jesus or His church. To plow up a hard heart—to experience God's love—hard hearted people need to be with people who love Jesus. And one of the best natural ways of getting enough time with someone who has a hard heart, so that they may *see* the Good News, is to work with them six or more hours a day.

When people experience grace, forgiveness and love day in and day out, week in and week out, month in and month out, they have no explanation. They have no answer to their "Why?" Like the magicians in Moses' time who had solutions and answers in the beginning but who over time ran out of answers, our coworkers become convinced and exclaim—"THIS IS THE FINGER OF GOD!"[3]

I've learned from my own experience—and from that of hundreds of B4T workers—that the first ten to twenty times when people who know nothing of Jesus experience His love, grace and forgiveness through the ways we work, they simply assume we do not understand their language and culture. The next ten to forty times when these same people realize our language is okay and we do in fact grasp their culture, they begin to wonder if we are just stupid. The way we live and the way we work make no sense to them. But somewhere between the twentieth and ninetieth times (and that usually takes one or more years), they connect the dots. They realize for themselves it is Jesus who makes us as we are, and it is then that things begin to change in their hearts and minds. Changing hearts and changing minds is the result of plowing deeply.

Often, those of us overseas tell the church back home, "These people are hard," or "The work is so difficult," but then we keep on *sowing*. In Mark 13 Jesus shouts to the crowds, LISTEN! PLEASE LISTEN! Because, as the crowd understood about sowing …

If you know that the soil is hard, you do not keep sowing. You start plowing!

If the soil is dry—water.

If the soil lacks nutrients—fertilize.

Yet in reality, what do we do? We keep sowing! And then there is no harvest, so we blame the soil or Satan. People with hard hearts close their ears to advice but open their eyes to example.

Missionaries are usually very good at TELLING what they have heard of Jesus. With evangelism, the emphasis often is on persuading people to come to Christ. However, a witness is someone who has experienced—both seen and heard something—and then reports it to another. If we only *talk* about Jesus, people often conclude we have not actually experienced Him. The point is we need to share who Jesus is through our words *and* actions.

If people are going to grasp the meaning and value of love, they need to see it and experience it. Love is not taught, it is caught. Love demands action. Working a job, day in and day out with people enables people to both see and experience God's love in our lives and observe the finger of God.

Daily Plowing

Hard hearts refer to people who have their eyes shut and their ears closed; so how do we open them? We do it with prayer and love, flowing through His Spirit within us. But words alone are not sufficient. Hearing about prayer and talking about love will not result in many coming to Jesus. For example, several Muslim friends have commented about how little Christians pray, because they never see us pray. Surely, we do not want to be like the Pharisees who flaunted their prayers as a witness of their own piety. However, we need to develop spiritual disciplines in our daily lives that include connecting with the Spirit's wisdom in all that we do. We need to deliberately plan actions of love into our daily routines. Every hard soil (heart) has its breaking point. We need to invest time reflecting with the Spirit on the choices and actions we make each day to ensure we are reflecting Christ-like love in a way people may understand. If we are going to break up hard ground, we need to plow with prayer and love.

Using a business illustration, if we are trying to sell a product where there is no market, what do we have to do first? We first need to create a market for the product. Keep in mind that it is not enough to tell customers how wonderful the product is. We must *demonstrate* for them how the product works and how it will make their life better. Jesus proclaims, *Neither do people light a lamp and put it under a bowl. Instead, they put it on its stand, and it gives light to everyone in the house. Let your light so shine before men so that they may see your good works and glorify God who is in heaven.*[4] Just as people need to see the light for it to be meaningful, people also need to see and experience a new product before they will buy it.

If we are going to focus on reaching our neighbors, we need to give time for them to see and experience Jesus; we need to invest more than a few hours a week with them. The reason that the workplace is the ideal location for modeling the reality of God within us is two-fold: first, we are together for extended periods of time, and second, the best times for modeling the power of the Gospel do not necessarily happen when things are going well, but rather when things are stressful or even falling apart.

When things are going well, Christians and non-Christians alike respond similarly—we all feel life is good. But what about when the office is flooded or destroyed by an earthquake, or a client is overdue in paying for goods or services, or a government official wants a bribe for the fourth time? What if an employee lies to you, or steals from you, or continues to show up late for work? In those instances, when we extend grace or forgiveness we model how our faith allows us to respond differently. When we respond to hatred with love, people experience the distinctives of our beliefs. Trials, difficulties; these create opportunities for people to experience God working in our lives. Non-believers see how love operates in us when we face difficult situations. It is in these times that the difference between Jesus and politics, Jesus and science, Jesus and the Quran and the Mahayana Sutras and the Hindu Vedas come alive for them. It is in these hard times that they recognize something is different *within* us. Non-believers see and experience Jesus, and not just religion.

There is a well-known expression in English—*talk is cheap*. In other words, don't tell me, show me. Demonstrate the truth, the reality, of what is being said. The real impact, the lasting value, comes from living out the Gospel so our co-workers and friends can experience it.

Plowing is most impactful when people see ...

- How we respond to troubles and tough times—hearts and attitudes toward Jesus change.
- How we reach out to and bless them when they face troubles of their own—love is cultivated in their hearts.
- How we go the second mile to bless strangers or competitors—grace is watered into their minds.

- How we deal with those who treat us badly—forgiveness is fertilized into their souls.

When business or life is going great, there isn't much difference between the attitudes of Christians and non-Christians. It is in our difficulties, the tough times, that Christians respond differently with faith, hope, joy and love; that is when His light shines brightest through us. It is when it is darkest that the littlest of lamps shine brightest.

Bearing Fruit

Does plowing prayer and love work? Does the time we invest, even ten thousand hours, really make a difference?

At the OPEN Connect 2016, (a meeting for OPEN Network members, held every other year) I asked the one hundred and ninety OPEN workers who were all living and working in unreached areas, *"How many of you have been working for one to three years, at least twenty hours a week, in a hard soil? Please stand up."* Roughly fifty to sixty people stood.

I continued, *"Now if you have already had a co-worker say something like, 'Working here is better than any other place I've ever worked,' or, 'I really enjoy working with you,' please sit down."* Nearly everyone sat down.

In farming the Gospel, the first three years of plowing are hard. A plowing machine goes deeper into the soil than a harvest machine. In ministry, plowing digs into co-workers, customers and even into you. You cannot expect fruit when plowing. Plowing is the first step towards bearing fruit when we harvest. Having co-workers or employees make the above statements tells us we have cracked the surface. But these co-workers or employees are not yet ready for the seed. If we plant the seed at this point, they will wind up as seed sown on stony or thorny ground. When co-workers or employees ask, "Why do you do this?" Or "why do you care?" It shows that we are moving in the right direction. However, it is still too early to sow the seed of the Gospel. If you want lasting results, be patient. People are watching, so keep loving, keep modeling the Gospel, keep plowing.

Once the surface of unbelief is cracked, then up come the stones—the person's character and self-image. Some of my employees over the years thought nothing of taking home staplers, books, pens, money left on a counter, or any other item within their reach. It is our responsibility to teach our co-workers integrity, honesty and excellence. Model these qualities for them. Our actions are more influential than our words. As people grow in their personal integrity, their work will reflect it. They may not comment, but you will observe it because as human beings become more righteous, their own self-esteem begins to improve too. Their lives begin to heal. Do not expect this to happen in a few weeks, or even months. Our experience has taught us that the change happens quicker if you are working in your native country and in your native language. Yet note that it still might take a year or two working daily with people before the ground becomes soft. Remember that soft soil is not necessarily fertile soil; there are also different types of hard soil. Solid rock may require dynamite, whereas other hard soil may simply need a good working over with a spade. Prayer, and the Spirit's discernment are key in knowing what is needed to penetrate the heart of each person.

Next, we confront the weeds and thorns. This is the tougher concept for two reasons. First, there are many temptations in this world, and each person has different weaknesses. Second, there are a lot of pressures from family, culture and history. Since we cannot know which weaknesses and pressures each person faces, we must rely on the Holy Spirit to be at work to transform them. Our job is to pray and love. Pray for our co-workers whenever we think of them and pray before and during our times of interacting together. Ask Jesus for ways and opportunities to demonstrate His love for people in our normal daily routines. Invest in co-workers this way and the Holy Spirit will use it to prepare them to receive His seed.

Once you have been working together for one, maybe three years, it is at this stage that your co-workers often begin to ask you about your faith. Even without your mentioning Jesus directly to them for all those years, they will ask. They will likely ask for a copy of the Bible too. Why am I so certain? Experience. I also asked the OPEN workers at the OPEN Connect, *"If you've been working twenty plus hours per week, in the same business with roughly the same people for seven or more years, please stand up."* Exactly twenty people stood. (That reflects how young our movement is.) I continued, *"Now, if you or your team working with you has seen one or more persons come to faith, who are baptized, who are sticking with the faith, sit down."* Precisely eighteen of the twenty overseas professionals sat down. That means that after seven years ninety percent are seeing fruit: fruit that lasts.

In time, after three to five years, as you approach an investment of ten thousand hours with people, the soil is softened, the rocks are removed, the weeds are plowed under, and suddenly the soil is ready for the seed. It is encouraging to find that after the eight-year mark, business after business experiences breakthroughs in people coming to faith. Working side-by-side with people does bear fruit.

Being in the workplace positions us out in the harvest where we are constantly, yet naturally, required by our lives and actions to plow, cultivate, fertilize, water, and sow. In time we will reap a harvest. This requires patience. During those early years on the job, prioritize modeling the Gospel. Initially, when people ask you about your faith or your actions (and they will ask), they are likely curious but lack an urgency, or hunger, to know. Regularly point out to them that it is Jesus who causes you to be different. Be patient there is no rush to share more. Wait until you sense an eagerness, a hunger in their comments and questions. Do not be in a hurry to share your testimony or a tract until there is an exigency from them to hear about Jesus. It is the urgency in people that tells us the soil is ready to receive the seed. When people insist, even beg to know His Truth, that is the moment when the soil is ready for the seed.

For the message of the Kingdom to germinate and flourish in a person's mind and heart, preparations are necessary. An unprepared soil struggles to receive the seed. An unprepared heart struggles to receive the Word of God. When people ask questions about your upright or godly actions, simply point them to Jesus. Say things like, "I do it because of Jesus," or "Jesus wants me to do this." Identify your actions with Jesus, honor Him and point to Him, but there is no need to say anything more. Wait. To reemphasize, wait for the soil to be ready. It is when there is an urgency, a hunger, in a person's asking, that is when we know the soil is ready for the seed—the seed that will bear lasting fruit.

Plowing prayer and plowing love in hard ground and hard hearts will test your limits. Farming requires endurance. Endurance is a fruit of the Spirit. Remember that living for Jesus in our workplace is not only about reaching people for Christ. The work Jesus has assigned to us also requires us to follow His example, enabling Him to work within us to develop the fruits of His Spirit. And yes, Jesus is also working through us to impact the lives of those around us. He is working both in us and through us for His glory.

Embrace the need to endure. DON'T QUIT! Your plowing is likely making cracks in the soil. The visible evidence will be the improvement of the character of those you work with. Maybe some non-religious friends will become more aware of their words or actions. In the Muslim world it is common to see co-workers become better Muslims because of our lives at work. That is ok! It is a good sign that our plowing is making an impact.

Nathan is a good friend of mine. I knew him before he moved overseas and I visited him at least once every year when he was abroad. He had been working faithfully five, six days a week to start and build a language center in a neglected part of a huge city. The business had some hard times in the beginning. His family had struggles too. But he remained committed. After his fifth year, the business, family, *everything*, started to come together, and by year eight the business was really humming. Nathan was interacting with scores of people, plowing up the rocks and weeds, doing a great job of modeling the Gospel. But there was one problem: no sign of spiritual fruit. I paid him a visit and he complained, "All this work and what have I to show for it? I feel like a farmer planting flowers in the desert: there's nothing to show for all this effort." We discussed how God might not have brought him here to win Muslims to Jesus, but perhaps to teach him something. He smiled and replied, "Yes, I sure have changed since moving here." A few days later I left and Nathan went back to work. The next email I received from Nathan telling how Adul, his office manager, had come to Christ. Before he sold the business to another B4T worker, Nathan saw a handful of Muslim co-workers and clients introduced to Jesus.

We cannot plow hard ground in a day. Again, I emphasize: **Plowing prayer and plowing love in hard ground and hard hearts will test your limits.** I believe this challenge is a big part of our maturing process—growing in Christ. Endurance results in God's blessings.[5]

People will not change by being told to change. People need to experience His presence through our lives. I have consulted with professionals living and working in arid places like China, Egypt, Morocco and southeastern California, where the physical lands have been transformed and turned into lush productive farmland. With God's help, I believe we can accomplish the same in spiritual deserts. The key lies in how we cultivate the soil. If you have been out there working three, four, or five years, endure and cling to the hope that the harvest is coming. Keep plowing, for the harvest will happen! You need to persevere, so that when you have done the will of God, you will receive what he has promised.[6]

Summary

"Isaac planted crops in that land and the same year reaped a hundredfold, because the Lord blessed him. The man became rich, and his wealth continued to grow until he became very wealthy."[7] As Jesus pointed out in the Parable of the Sower, are we working the soil diligently so as to

see thirty, sixty, or a hundredfold results? Prayer and Love are key. Patience and perseverance are needed.

Plowing and sowing the Gospel into people's lives require time and consistency. In plowing, our evangelistic strategies and tools are all meant to be helpful, but they are not straitjackets, nor magic wands. In order to recalibrate missions, we need to keep our focus on Jesus and not rely on our own ideas.

Doing business puts all of us out into the fields where we are constantly, yet naturally required by our life and actions to plow, sow, cultivate, water, and—over time—reap. When we *plow*, our co-workers observe our actions—they begin to change their mindset about Jesus or Christians.

Bottom line, Jesus opens hearts and minds and He usually works through us. Our lives and work are all about Jesus: nothing more, nothing less. He is not just the most important piece in the puzzle of plowing and sowing the Gospel; He *is* the puzzle. He may choose for us to bear fruit in seven years—maybe fewer or maybe more. Whatever the time frame; stay at the plow. No matter how dark or how stormy life becomes, keep to His path; press on in cutting furrows. Plow in prayer. Plow in love. Be continually involved with on-going relationships. Be with the same hard-hearted people day in and day out—work with them. If we do our jobs, God will give the growth.[8]

9

WORK REVISITED, WORSHIP RECALIBRATED

The world hates change, yet it is the only thing that has brought progress.
—Charles Kettering

We need a revolution every generation or so. —Thomas Jefferson

What is truth? —Pontius Pilate

I am the way the truth and the life. —Jesus

———

CALIBRATION IS a comparison between two instruments. Put simply, calibration is the process of comparing the measured value from an instrument under calibration with a reference or standard of known and high accuracy. What we are doing in this book is comparing the values we hold high in the church and mission and comparing them with the Word of God. Calibrating our lives, work, and faith against the words of God is essential because we need to get an accurate measurement of what we believe and how we live out those beliefs.

My former mentor, Phil Parshall when asked, "What is a balanced life?" replied, "Balance is where I am at." This is so true. Most of us consider our lives to be balanced and the lives of others to be out of balance. The fulcrum for most of us is ourselves. We tend to form our own realities and those realities are not perfect. Self-perception can be very limiting. It is easy to become locked into certain perceptions, get stuck in routines and lose sight of differing viewpoints hindering us from understanding the truth. Nonetheless, shaking up our notions of the world—including life and work—can do wonders for our growth, productivity and happiness.

The Power of Being One

The phrase *one another* occurs one hundred times in the New Testament. Approximately 59 of those occurrences are specific commands teaching us how and how not to relate to *one another*. The phrase *one another* is derived from the Greek word ἀλλήλων (allélón). *Allélón* is a reciprocal pronoun most often translated in the Bible as *one another* and indicates that two or more people are carrying out, or have carried out, an action of some type, with all receiving simultaneously the benefits or consequences of that action. There is a sense to *allélón* of togetherness, mutual benefit, or oneness. Jesus and every New Testament author uses the word to express oneness.

In John 17:11 & 21, Jesus prays that His followers may *be one*. Here He is using the word ἓν (εἷς), the literal number "one" in Hebrew. Yet again, Jesus is emphasizing in His prayers for us His concern that we be *one*. Oneness appears to be an important concept to Jesus and to each of the New Testament authors.

Allélón is used in Hebrews 10:24-25, where we are encouraged *not to neglect meeting together*. In other words, Christians are to meet together regularly. In meeting together, we are to practice the "one anothers" of the Bible: serving one another,[1] loving one another,[2] praying for one another,[3] teaching one another,[4] etcetera. In practicing the "one anothers," we demonstrate God's love to the world.[5] Acts 2 is a powerful example of this. There we see the early *ekklesia* (church) coming together in love and practicing the *one another* verses in love. The result? *And the Lord added to their number daily those who were being saved.*[6] Our lives in Jesus are meant to be one. There is no dichotomy between my job, my marriage, my exercise, my vacations, my church work, and so on.

If we are sincerely worshipping God in all aspects of life, we will certainly worship when we get together. Romans 12:1 is a well-known example of Paul using worship-related words in some surprising ways: *I urge you, brothers, in view of God's mercy, to offer your bodies as living* **sacrifices***, holy and pleasing to God—this is your spiritual act of worship.* Worship is the giving of our entire selves, our thoughts and our emotions, for God's use. Jesus states it this way: *If any man will come after me, let him deny himself and take up his cross and follow me.*[7] Paul clarified this when he penned, *I am crucified with Christ: nevertheless I live; yet not I, but Christ lives in me.*[8] Christ and Paul are *one*; Christ and all believers are *one*.

The Bible teaches that all of life is an act of submission, an act of worship to Jesus. And all of life includes our work, our play, our study. Whatever we do, whether in words or actions, we are to do all things in the name of the Lord Jesus.[9] This includes our time and our attitudes and actions with our spouse, kids, co-workers, and neighbors. Our service, or *avodah* to God, is not centered on a time or a temple. It is to be done whenever and wherever we are because we *are* the temple of God.[10] We take the emphasis away from ceremony, seasons, places, and rituals, and we shift it to what is happening inside of us. Worship should invade our entire lives in all places and at all times. The test of worship is not only what happens at church, but what happens at home, at work and wherever God places us.

Every act of obedience is an act of worship. It declares that God has worth. And whenever we share the gospel with someone, we are declaring God's worth. We are engaging in the priestly service of preaching the Gospel. Our bodies are temples of the Living God, making our lives the worship of being witnesses to God's grace. When we tell people what a great thing God has done in Jesus Christ and how that has been good news in our lives, we are declaring His worth. In this way, whatever we do we are giving Him worship.[11] We do not have to wait for a church service. We do not have to have a Bible in our hands and we certainly do not need clergy to be present.

We get our English word "liturgy" from the Greek word *leitourgia*. In the Greek Septuagint,[12] and in pagan Greek literature, the word refers to public works of worship. But Paul used it in a different context—*an offering of money.* He uses this word for worship to describe financial help: money to be used in helping other Christians in famine relief, or money to be used in helping spread the Gospel. Romans 15:27 uses this word: *If the Gentiles have shared in the Jews' spiritual blessings, they owe it to the Jews to minister to them*—literally, to give liturgy to them—*with material blessings.* Giving material blessing, including money, is a seemingly ordinary service that we do for others. However, clearly giving was considered an act of worship—a God-approved, religious activity.

After receiving financial help from the church in Philippi Paul further wrote: *I have received full payment and even more; I am amply supplied, now that I have received from Epaphroditus the gifts you sent. They are a fragrant* offering, *an acceptable* sacrifice, *pleasing to God.*[13] And to the church in Corinth he wrote, *This service*—this liturgy—*that you perform is not only supplying the needs of God's people but is also over-flowing in many expressions of thanks to God.*[14] Both of these churches were worshipping God with their money. This is the foundation for understanding why nearly every church today views the giving of tithes and offerings as a form of worship.

The Old Testament law required the Israelites to serve God through His established priesthood. The priests were to offer sacrifices in the temple on behalf of the people. Jesus fulfilled the law.[15] With the law fulfilled, all believers became priests.[16] In Jesus, there is no need for others to intercede for us. The temple veil was torn, giving all believers priesthood status; the ministry of worship has been given to all His people. This changes worship dramatically. God's temple is on the move, literally going wherever a believer goes.

We are to worship God wherever we go, doing all things to God's glory, praying always, giving thanks always,[17] never ceasing to be a temple of the Holy Spirit.[18] Worship is not restricted to a specific place and time. Although we are meant to worship all the time, we also worship together at *specific* times and at meetings designated for that specific purpose. Our worship involves how and where we work, how we interact with others and how we choose what to watch on TV and online—everything! *For God is not so unjust as to overlook your work and the love which you showed for his sake in serving the saints, as you still do.*[19]

Hebrews 13 combines two New Testament forms of worship. *Through Jesus, therefore, let us continually offer to God a sacrifice of praise, the fruit of lips that confess his name. And do not forget to do good and to share with others, for **with such sacrifices** God is pleased.*[20] Worship involves words of praise and acts of service to others. Whether those acts of doing good are done within a church, within the community, or within our places of work, they are sacrifices of worship and pleasing to God.

We need to recalibrate. If we are one in Christ and if our money (our financial offerings) is accepted as liturgy (as a form of worship), then our work must also be considered a form of worship. The clergy readily grasp and remind us when we attend church that giving our tithes and monies as an offering to the church is worship. So now our clergy need to understand that the Scriptures advocate that designing a website, flying a plane, constructing a house and doing housework are also forms of worship. Preachers can stop telling us to quit our jobs to go into the ministry because in God's eyes doing our jobs *is* a form of ministry. Why are Sunday church meetings called "worship services" and our nine to five job is not? If we recalibrate to God's perspective of work, our so-called secular work (nine-to-five job) can be considered sacred (worship service), just as sacred as our weekly church meetings are.

Work is Worship

Jesus is clear:

- *All authority in heaven and on earth has been given to me. Therefore go and make disciples of all nations, baptizing them in the name of the Father and of the Son and of the Holy Spirit, and teaching them to obey everything I have commanded you.*[21]
- *As the Father has sent me, I am sending you.*[22]
- *But you will receive power when the Holy Spirit comes on you; and you will be my witnesses in Jerusalem, and in all Judea and Samaria, and to the ends of the earth.*[23]

We should apply these verses—and many others like them—in our daily lives and work. Since the majority of us spend nearly one-third of our time in our place of work, it should be our primary site for working out our salvation[24] and witnessing to people—even to the ends of the earth. Our jobs should never stand in the way of our walk with Jesus. Rather, our places of work should reflect our spirituality and thus bear witness to those around us. Our work should demonstrate what it means to have a relationship with God.

When we grasp God's intention for work, from Genesis to Revelation, we realize work is meant to be relational and transformational, drawing others to His Throne. However, normally we are taught to think of worship as something we do at church, primarily on Sunday, and work as something we do Monday through Friday. For example, how many believers in the "secular work force" wake up Monday morning with a prayer or the mindset of, "Jesus, I'm going to my ministry, where You have placed me to be Your salt and light to my co-workers and customers?" This dichotomy is neither what God designed for our lives, nor what He desires.

For centuries, the church has viewed pastoral and missionary work as being the most spiritual way of serving God and others. Such "full-time ministries" seem to be granted greater spiritual value than secular occupations, even though they are not expressly compared in that way. We trust those holding secular jobs to fund those doing the "real ministry," and at the same time our perception is that they have precious few moments outside of weekends or evenings to do "ministry" by being Sunday School teachers, elders, greeters, musicians, etcetera. While these structured or formal church ministries are not misguided efforts, something is wrong with the disconnect between "ministry" and the workplace.

Understanding Work

Work is defined as "exertion or effort directed to produce or accomplish something."[25] Therefore, what we strive to achieve may be considered "work." This is the framework for Paul telling the church in Ephesus, *serve wholeheartedly, as if you were serving the Lord, not people, because you know that the Lord will reward each one for whatever good they do, whether they are slave or free.*[26]

Our work is a witness. Good work is a good witness; bad work is a bad witness. I am reminded of an example of bad witnessing when, thirty years ago, my sister said to me, "I am not going to church any more. My landlady goes to church all the time, but after five weeks of multiple requests, she's too busy going to church to fix my broken window." People examine the reality of our faith by what we do, not by what we say.

"You are serving the Lord not people." In its simplest sense, we do all

things "to the glory of God." This means that our actions and words should display a pure heart through which God accomplishes His work. Our work is to reflect God and be a means of His glorifying Himself through us. The integration of work and worship is *workship.*

The way in which we do our jobs impacts lives and can turn people either away from, or toward Jesus. The workplace may be one of the most misunderstood fields for the Gospel, whether that be in India or Indiana. Our work contributes to the growth and progress of society. If we are going to improve our impact among the unreached, we need to start with who we are and how we are discipled at home. Those in professional church work need to increase their understanding of the world of work. On more than one occasion a pastor has asked me, "How can I better relate to the businesspeople in my congregation?" My answer is simple: "Get a job in the marketplace. Learn how to work as others work. Learn how to be a witness in the workplace and then teach your congregants to be witnesses in the workplace."

Workship includes giving God the best of what He has given to us. Whenever God blesses, fills, touches, or surprises us, we need to give those gifts back to Him as an offering, a gift of thanks for His goodness to us. As we live a life of workship, everything we possess—time, things, thoughts—should be celebrated as gifts from Him. God's blessings are to be shared. If we hoard His blessings for ourselves, they will become rotten, just as the manna did when the people hoarded it.[27] We must share His blessings with others and with them bring Him glory. We know from the story of the Good Samaritan, that "others" is not limited to other Christians. Being Jesus's salt and light to co-workers requires us to be out among the people who have yet to meet Jesus.

Oneness is important to God. In Genesis 12:8 we read about Abraham: *He moved from there to the mountain east of Bethel, and he pitched his tent with Bethel on the west and Ai on the east; there he built an altar to the Lord and called on the name of the Lord.*

Oswald Sanders wrote the following in his commentary on this verse:

> *Bethel is the symbol of fellowship with God; Ai is the symbol of the world. Abram "pitched his tent" between the two. The lasting value of our public service for God is measured by the depth of the intimacy of our private times of fellowship and oneness with Him. Rushing in and out of worship is wrong every time— there is always plenty of time to worship God. Days set apart for quiet can be a trap, detracting from the need to have daily quiet time with God. That is why we must "pitch our tents" where we will always have quiet times with Him, however noisy our times with the world may be. There are not three levels of spiritual life—worship, waiting and work. Yet some of us seem to jump like spiritual frogs from worship to waiting and from waiting to work. God's idea is that the three should go together as one. They were always together in the life of our Lord and in perfect harmony. It is a discipline that must be developed; it will not happen overnight.*[28]

Work and worship are not viewed as separate duties or entities in Scripture, any more than we view our soul as separate from our pumping hearts. We cannot separate our soul and our hearts; we likewise should not separate our daily lives from our daily worship. God does not treat us as disconnected parts. He views us—all that we are and all that we do—as one.

My good friend, Mats Tunehag, explains the notion of *workship* well:

> *Business as Mission is about making our Sunday talk into a Monday walk. Whatever we believe and profess in church on Sunday should be permeating our lives and business practices the rest of the week. But we must strive towards a seamless integration of Sunday and Monday, of work and worship. There is a risk of seeing Sunday and Monday as two separate compartments. There are pros and cons with compartmentalization. It has been a key to scientific development. But*

the danger is often that one may fail to see the greater whole; how bits and pieces overlap, interact and connect.

For example, H_2O is hydrogen and oxygen. It can be compartmentalized and analyzed and it can manifest itself as water, ice and steam. Worship in the temple is different from manual labor in the field. But that doesn't mean that they are disconnected from who we are, created in God's image, with a purpose to both work and worship. Work can be worship. We must avoid playing one important entity against the other. It is not hydrogen versus oxygen, God the Father versus the Son, work versus worship, or the financial bottom-line versus a spiritual impact. They are not the same, but they belong together. Thus, our daily work is intimately related to serving God and people. Our businesses are not a distraction from "doing ministry."[29]

For many, the workplace is the focal point of our life. We get our identity from our jobs. We take pride in the work we do and the successes we achieve. The workplace is also the place where our limitations, our fears and our egoism are revealed to us. It is a place where our true, sinful self surfaces. Because it is real, people can relate to us. The workplace is a place where people are often very open to meeting God. We need to strive both to teach and to model for people how prayer and worship can occur as naturally and frequently within the office, the classroom, the factory, and all other places of work.

Summary

Workship. Work of any kind, if done unto God, is worship. We need to realign our vocabulary to fit with Scripture. We should calibrate the ways we have become like the Pharisees in creating vocabulary and practices with which we are comfortable and yet have claimed are Biblical. For example, if our nine-to-five job is worship, then what is Sunday morning church? Should we rename "the worship service," calling it a "praise service" or "celebration service?"

Jesus prays for us to be one. This applies to church communities, our neighborhoods and our places of employment. Our religious beliefs and practices cannot be separated from other areas of our lives.

What needs to be recalibrated? The compartmentalized view we have of life and work. We do not live life in a collection of boxes. We are wholly one, striving to serve a holy God. We need to worship both inside *and* outside the walls of our churches. We need to workship.

10

NEW WINESKINS FOR NEW WINE

Change is the law of life. And those who look only to the past or present are certain to miss the future. —John F. Kennedy

The best way to predict the future is to invent it. —Peter Drucker

When it is evening, you say, 'It will be fair weather; for the sky is red.' And in the morning, 'It will be stormy today, for the sky is red and threatening.' You know how to interpret the appearance of the sky, but you cannot interpret the signs of the times. —Jesus

---

Two Illustrations

IN THE ANCIENT world the wine press was a large basin where men would tread grapes. They would hold on to ropes above them and stamp on the grapes with their feet. The juice would run into containers on the sides of the large basin. The juice was then poured into fresh goatskins to ferment. These goatskins were tied off at the legs and hung from the rafters by a hook placed just below the neck of each goatskin. The goatskins were a perfect container to ferment the grapes. As the grape juice fermented, it would expand, and the fresh skins readily stretched to accommodate the juice. Depending on the temperature and the amount of yeast added to the juice within the goatskin, the juice would take 7 to 30 days to ferment. As the goatskin expanded with the juice, the outer skin would also harden. After a week or more, this hardened skin served as a perfect storage container for the wine and allowed for easy pouring into smaller jugs which could then be placed on a table.

At a time when John the Baptist's disciples and some Pharisees were fasting, *Some people came and asked Jesus, "How is it that John's disciples and the disciples of the Pharisees are fasting, but yours are not?"*[1] Jesus answered them with two brief illustrations.

He said:

No one tears a piece out of a new garment to patch an old one. Otherwise, they will have torn the new garment, and the patch from the new will not match the old. And no one pours new wine into old wineskins. Otherwise, the new wine will burst the skins; the wine will run out and the wineskins will be ruined. No, new wine must be poured into new wineskins. And no one after drinking old wine wants the new, for they say, 'The old is better.'[2]

The point is clear, the old ways and the new ways do not mix. To take a patch from a new garment to replace the old is foolish, as to do so would ruin the new garment. And as the old cloth has likely faded over time, the new patch would stand out and not match with the old.

In a similar way, if one pours new wine into an old wineskin, then as the wine ferments, the hardened skin could not adapt to the changing wine, resulting in the wineskin cracking. This would result in both the wine and the wineskin being wasted.

When new cultural or sociological transitions occurred throughout history, God raised up new generations and new strategies for spreading His glory in order to meet the new challenges. Each new paradigm took the Gospel deeper into those yet-to-be-reached areas and peoples of the world. Each transition played a role—a valuable role—in spreading the Gospel to where it was yet unknown; the Jesuits (the new worlds), William Carey (denominational missions), Hudson Taylor (faith missions & inland missions), OM & YWAM (short-terms missions), Frontiers & Pioneers (unreached people groups).

We all agree that the times are changing again. In the past, the established methodologies and parachurch agencies could not adapt with the changing times. Often, they would adopt the new terminology of that day, but only as a veneer for keeping things the same. The question is, can parachurch agencies formed in the *modern world* of the 19th and 20th centuries make the deep root changes needed to adjust to the opportunities and needs of *postmodern* 21st century?

We must make another major paradigm shift in our efforts to reach the unreached. Roughly thirty-times as many missionaries go to reached people groups—where churches exist, and where they work with Christians—than go to unreached people groups—where there are few or no local believers. Far less go to the unengaged people groups, where there are no believers and no missionaries, reaching out to them.[3] Based on history, it comes as no surprise that established mission agencies place over 95% of their workers where they have always worked and where churches are established.[4] It's a new day; there's a new wine needing new wineskins, new structures and new processes. Mission agencies and parachurch organizations need more than a new paint job or adding a new wing to the current structure— most everything needs to be rebuilt. As Warrant Buffet puts it, "In a chronically leaking boat, energy devoted to changing vessels is more productive than energy devoted to patching leaks."

New Wine Skins—Changing Times

In the 1400s, the printing press broke the barriers of keeping information in the hands of a few, and the building of larger ships opened up an age of exploration. These new inventions enabled the birth of the premodern world. For the first time ideas and goods could be taken, literally, to the ends of the earth. With the invention of the steam engine, the entrepreneurs of the early 1800s began to build steam-powered ships and trains. At nearly the same time, the telegraph came into being. Thus began the modern world and the industrial revolution. These inventions allowed ideas and goods to move rapidly and for far greater distances. And then along came the internet and the start of the postmodern world.

The 21st century is the century of change. The invention of the push button telephone, electric typewriters and transistor radios were all the rage of my youth. Where are they today? Today I carry in my pocket an invention that does all the things those inventions of my youth did, and much more. In the next decade, more things will change in more places than in the previous century. Change is often painful. Growth is often painful. But nothing is more painful than being stuck somewhere you do not belong. Change is no longer optional.

Jesus understands change and our preference for keeping things the same.[5] Yet throughout His time on earth, He kept breaking traditions and paradigms. He tells the leaders of His day:

When evening comes, you say, 'It will be fair weather, for the sky is red' and in the morning, 'Today it will be stormy, for the sky is red and overcast.' You know how to interpret the appearance of the sky, but you cannot interpret the signs of the times.[6]

How are we doing in our adjusting to the postmodern world?

Forty years ago, as a young missionary in a mission agency, I was taught to see the world as being built around walls. Missionaries are sent out to share the Gospel by overcoming walls and building bridges over these divisive walls. Missionaries are taught to look for ways to "contextualize" or "connect" or "build bridges" to the unreached so as to make the Gospel understandable in what is an unbiblical or foreign culture. Yet as the world is changing, so must our ways of sharing the Gospel change too.

Seeing is Believing

In July 1969, Neil Armstrong became the first man to walk on the moon. One of the best kept secrets of his moon walk is that while testing the moon's soil he heard the Islam call to prayer and upon returning to earth, studied Islam and ultimately became a Muslim.

... Fake news is everywhere. Yet thousands of uneducated Muslims believe this fifty years later.[7]

When I was younger and planned to take my wife out for a meal, I would ask around to find what restaurants my friends recommended. Young people today still ask around when choosing a place for dinner, but more likely they are going to go online and check several restaurants' reviews. Due to the plethora of fake news, people check the facts before moving forward with deciding. When people hear the Gospel, they do the same thing. They search around to find out what is true. Yet with all the misinformation about the Gospel and the Bible online, who and what are people going to believe? Our words, or example? Do those we are sharing with know us well enough to trust our words and examples more than what they read and hear elsewhere? How Christ-like is our daily living?

We know there is often a gap between the average Christian's once-a-week church activity and how they live Christ's life in the workplace. In a similar way, those of us who are focused on evangelism also have a gap between our evangelistic efforts and how we contextualize or live out the Gospel with our co-workers and neighbors. Evangelism should not be an activity that we "perform" periodically, but a constant outflow of our daily routine. In addition, our vocabulary and our physical appearance not only needs to fit in with those we are reaching out to, but our actions at home and in our workplace should be the same as our actions in the church. Such consistency reflects His glory and releases a wholeness and a harmony which fulfills our God-given mandate to be a witness for Him in all we do.[8] Jesus ministered in the marketplace. Jesus ministered in the synagogue. So should we. The culture will not be transformed unless it happens through us.

The following story is an example of what can happen when we only *teach* people the truth of the Gospel but do not *live out* the truth of the Gospel among them.

> *The audience quieted down. Her countenance was heavy with sorrow. "I am from the country that has been considered by many of you to be the greatest example of success in world missions," she began. She told how the church was planted over a century ago, and how today 85 percent of the people call themselves Christians. Much of the growth came from evangelical and Pentecostal churches, which exceed 25 percent of the total. Excitement grew in the hall as she described high interest in Bible study and prayer.*
>
> *But then she asked, "Do any of you know where I am from?" Many guesses were called out, all of which were wrong. She finally said: "I am from Rwanda—the same country in which, in 1994, 600,000 Tutsis and 400,000 Hutus died, many of them slaughtered with machetes as they huddled in churches. In all of your zeal for evangelism, you brought us Christ but never taught us how to live."*
>
> *If the end is in sight, how do we explain Rwanda, as well as other so-called Christian countries where unrestrained materialism, oppression of the underprivileged, and deterioration of moral values increase annually? Surely these are not the consequences envisioned by our Lord when he said, "Go and make disciples ... teaching them to obey everything I have commanded you."[9] To put it bluntly, something has gone wrong with the harvest.[10]*

One of my students who was present in Rwanda before and after the genocide agrees. He told me that "Christianity was a religion accepted by the people. They had learned the trappings of the religion. They copied what they saw the missionaries doing, but they had never internalized their faith into their daily activities."

Jesus-loving, for-profit businesses have much to offer and teach charitable societies. Charitable services are most needed in moments of emergencies; but in many cases, the long-term dependency which these organizations foster do not bring hope and new life to the people. Contrastingly, the dignity which real work gives people, along with the hourly conversations and examples which these interactions provide, brings a much higher level of openness to the truths and hope of the Gospel. Christian businesses often have interns and apprentices who may render services alongside the businesses—services that frequently mimic traditional charitable services—but the intent of these services should be to receive training and knowledge/education in how to best bless and share the love of Jesus in real life, in natural daily encounters. Jesus invested much of his time and teaching near and among the business community. Jesus did this without any intent of receiving anything in return. He modeled for us the importance of taking His Word into the everyday life and work of the people.

Clearly one reason poverty continues in places like Haiti—despite all the Christian relief efforts—and genocide could occur between two majority evangelical Christian peoples like the Hutus and Tutsis in Rwanda, is because the values and teaching of Jesus were never absorbed into the everyday life and work of the people. Rather, the people practice Christianity as a religion that is separated from their daily life and work rather than as a relationship with God which impacts and influences their moment-by-moment decisions and actions. A key to bringing about lasting change to communities is to model the Gospel (the life of Jesus) in those places where it is often neglected or unknown. When we bring the transforming power of God out of the church buildings and into all areas of society, including the workplace, then people may not only see, but also experience the true peace and love of Jesus.

Just like professionals at home, professionals working cross-culturally do not need to build bridges into the community because our jobs imbed us in the community. Business-for-transformation workers do not need to look for ways to "connect" or "contextualize," as our jobs connect and contextualize us effortlessly. Our position in society is understandable to people, making our life and witness more understandable as well. Non-Christians, Christians, everyone, no matter the job or employer, can grasp God's authority and power when they see work done in a way that glorifies Jesus. Having a job is a holy invitation to claim lives for the Kingdom.

But there is a warning that we all must heed no matter how we are seeking to share the Gospel. As the next story displays, the moment we stop looking to God at each step of our life and work is the moment our witness changes from a living testimony into a dead method. I fear this has happened in many established evangelistic agencies; and if we are not careful, we could turn the BAM and B4T movements into a dry, step-by-step method as well.

Consider King David. In his first decade of leadership, every time David goes into battle he talks to God and asks what he should do, and then he does it. And he wins every battle. He has a perfect record. Then there is the episode with the Ark. David enlists the priests and brothers, Uzzah and Ahio, to bring the Ark back to Jerusalem. We can assume these are David's friends, men who serve him well. They build a new cart for transporting the Ark and are rewarded with the honor of leading the procession of over 30,000 people to bring the Ark home to the City of David. But in route, the oxen stumble and Uzzah grabs the Ark to keep it from slipping off the cart. Touching the Ark was forbidden in the Law of God; transporting the Ark on a cart pulled by animals was also forbidden. Uzzah and Ahio as priests should have known this. So, for his attempt to help God stabilize His Ark, Uzzah is slain. Ouch! And David is furious.

Yes, David is mad at God. Three months pass. David continues to fight battles, and he continues to win, but his relationship with God begins to change. He stops asking God for permission and directions as he did in the past. Too often there is a familiarity that comes from doing things successfully over and over. As a result, it is not long before David chooses Bathsheba over leading his men into battle.[11]

Soon his house is divided, not once but twice, and his perfect record has a blemish as he flees Jerusalem.

Why have we not succeeded in reaching our communities and the unreached? Could it be because we are bringing the Gospel to the people on a cart pulled by oxen and not on the poles carried by Levites? Could it be that we have devised well-intended methodologies to win people to Jesus, but these are of our own design and desires and not His?

New Wineskins for the Post-Modern World—Changing Our Ways of Engagement

The history of civilization includes the story of business and technology development. From the wheel to the printing press, to the steam engine, to the internet, technology enables businesses to move and to market at a rapidly increasing pace. In the blink of an eye, companies can now take their products literally to every corner of the world.

As we look to the future and to spreading the Gospel, it is essential to understand the processes of change. One key factor is digitalization. Digitalization is driving the major breakthroughs of post-modernization. Digitalization enables us to quantify everything. Anything and everything can be counted. This fact has important cultural implications, as quantity is stressed over quality. Thus, those in Generation X and following usually value what can be counted and controlled. Yet as Ambassadors of the Good News, how do we count love? Discipleship is a relationship, not a program—how do we measure that? Yes, we may count disciples as the church once did among the Tutsis and Hutu of Rwanda, but are we counting/measuring the right metrics?

Marketing has obviously changed the way we live. However, it is also changing the way we value things, even ourselves. Marketing convinces us that we can be whatever we want to be. By becoming a product we are turning ourselves and everything around us into marketable goods. This is happening from Mumbai to Milwaukee, from Tehran to Tokyo. The world has not gotten smaller, it has gotten tiny. And everything that is measurable is dollar based. This new mentality affects our relationships, it impacts the way we work, it even alters the core values of our culture. Reality is becoming more and more subjective, more and more artificial. Science, not God, is calling the shots. And if you question that, consider the Covid-19 pandemic. Who were world leaders and even the vast majority of church leaders, looking to for guidance in dealing with the pandemic? Science.

As we look toward the future, what needs to be recalibrated? We need to understand how to build relationships in a digital world. Though life itself changes frequently, the workplace may become one stable rock that non-believers cling to for stability and security. If so, many of our evangelistic and missiological strategies need adjustments. We need to penetrate the marketplace.

When we first entered the postmodern world, the army promoted the idea of "An Army of One." Those who were marketing the Army tried to capture the individualized nature of the millennial generation. The idea was popular and after all the previous years of failure in meeting their recruitment goals, this ad campaign was successful.[12] As the army of God, what can we learn from the U.S. Army?

The Army's ad campaign demonstrates how the methods and roles of promoting ideas are changing. In the past, those who were marketing businesses, church ideas and the U.S. Army relied primarily on advertising through traditional mass media. Today, businesses and the U.S. Army are taking a different approach to spreading their message. Businesses and the Army now integrate their advertising efforts with a variety of communication techniques: social media, websites, direct marketing, sales promotion, publicity, and public relations, as well as sponsoring events in local communities. They are also recognizing that these communication tools are most effective when they are coordinated with other elements of the marketing program, especially their local recruiters.[13] The information and ideas used increases the number of personal touchpoints recruiters have with potential soldiers.

By definition, an army cannot be an individual. However, the Army discovered that each individual could retain his or her individual skills and personality, but still form a formidable army. Churches and parachurch organizations can learn from this. We need to recognize that God works with us as individuals; then we need to build on our individual giftings, education, experiences, and callings to disciple individuals into a beautiful mosaic of a community that glorifies God. The postmodern tools are not the solution; prayer and love in Jesus are the solution. Yet these tools will enhance our abilities to impact our communities for Christ.

Understand that for the Army, the tools assist in achieving their goals, but the tools are not the answer. There is still a need for that face-to-face relationship with someone on the ground. Thankfully, there is one shift in the church that is opening a way for believers to be better witnesses for Christ. The church, and some parachurch organizations, are willing to consider alternate ways of serving and witnessing. Nowadays there is also a fresh emphasis on listening and abiding in Jesus. We have learned that God speaks to everyone differently, meaning that each person's assignment is not going to be the same as anyone else's. That means outreach is becoming less and less about programs and events, and more about validating a person's calling and then working with the person to make God's assignment for them become a reality.

New Wineskins—Integrating Worship in Our Work & Words

The pastor of a large church was introducing the plenary speaker at the church's mission conference. "I've known Paul for nearly twenty years now. He's a member of our church who currently serves as the President of one of the largest mission organizations in the world. We have been privileged to be part of his support team for many years." The pastor continued, "Prior to Paul becoming a missionary, he worked as the Vice President (of a large local company), that is, until God called him and said, I have something bigger for you—a higher calling, at which time Paul left his career to become a missionary."

The pastor and the church were clearly proud of their missionary leader. But this is just one example of how unbiblical we have become. It demonstrates how there still is a "spiritual" hierarchy within the church. There is good and bad; spiritual and physical; sacred and secular; clergy and laity. This spiritual hierarchy suggests that in the body of Christ the pastors and church workers and missionaries are at the top followed by charity workers, and at the bottom are those making money in business. Mark Greene writes, "The overall marginalization of work is reflected in a belief within the church which goes something like this: 'All Christians are born equal, but full-time Christians are more equal than others.'"[14]

Even the term "full-time Christian worker" implies something, doesn't it? I was in China and was asked to meet an American who was serving as that country's leader for an international mission agency. I was asked to meet him by one of his staff who wanted to start a business but was meeting resistance. When the leader walked in the door, we shook hands and I immediately asked what he did for a living.

He smiled and replied, "I am a full-time Christian worker. What do you do?"

I grinned in return and answered, "I am a part-time Christian worker."

Obviously confused, he asked, "What's that mean?"

"Well," I said, "I run a business in addition to serving God; so if you're full-time, I must be a part-time Christian worker. But then, Jesus makes it clear we cannot be followers of Him on a part-time basis,[15] so I must be damned to hell; that's what it means."

Jesus had no problem calling out the hypocrites of His day, and we shouldn't either. I knew full well this Christian leader was in China on false pretenses, having a fake business. Like myself, just a decade before, he was calling people to the Truth, while he was lying daily about his reasons for being in the country. Yet he was blind to the lie he was living. Needless to add, soon afterward the staff member resigned so he could start what has become a successful B4T business touching many lives for Jesus with integrity.

"Full-time Christian worker" terminology is not biblical, yet it still dominates our thinking and behavior in the church and parachurch agencies. Every Christian is a full-time Christian. Every father is a full-time father. Every businessman is a full-time businessman. And every pastor is a full-time pastor. If you are pastor, call yourself a pastor. If you are a missionary, identify yourself as a missionary. There's no offense in that. We all have different giftings and assignments from the Lord. But whenever anyone says, "I am a full-time Christian worker," the implication is clearly a put down to all non-professional Christian workers. We are all priests.[16] Whatever job we have, we are all called to serve full-time in God's army.[17]

Some have told me, "If I told people I was a missionary I'd get kicked out of the country or maybe killed." Did the full-time Christians of Nero's day tell the Romans, "Whoa, don't send me to the Coliseum to face the lions, I'm only a part-time Christian?"

"Hypocrites!" I hear Jesus shouting. How can we expect Him to bless our ministries when we are lying to people about why we are there? If you are a missionary in the USA or wherever you are from, then you are a missionary in Pakistan or Iran, or wherever you are going.

As someone who has lived in a Muslim country for nearly half my life, I have never understood how missionaries can trust God to meet their financial needs, but they cannot trust God to meet their needs of physical safety. If He sends us, He will provide *and* protect us.[18] Psalm 34:19 tells us: *The righteous person may have many troubles, but the LORD delivers him from them all.* Whether we are employed by the church, parachurch or another business or organization, we all work for Jesus and His words apply to all of us. Wherever we serve Him, if we are lying—living an unrighteous life—then we cannot rely on His deliverance. But if we are striving to live righteously, we will have troubles, but in His time and His way, He will deliver us from them.

We should not compartmentalize our lives. When I am in my own house, I often am thinking about my work. When I am at work, I am often thinking about my boys. Yes, at different times of the day we each prioritize different aspects of who we are. We cannot change that. If I am at work, and my wife calls and says our son has just been hit by a car and taken to the hospital, am I going to tell her, "Honey, you know I am at work now, can we talk about this when I get home?" No, I am going to drop everything and rush to the hospital. Likewise, if I am reading to my kids in bed at night, and I get a call that one of our employees has been severely injured in a car accident, am I going to say, "Sorry, can you call me during office hours?" No, I am going to get up and rush out to help.

God calls us to an integrated life, not a prioritized life. Many Christians like to say, "My priority is God first, family second, and my work third." Really? Then why do you spend more time at work than with your family? We can pull verses out of context to prove these points; but does God agree? One verse people often throw out when they prioritize this way is 1 Timothy 5:8, *Anyone who does not provide for their relatives, and especially for their own household, has denied the faith and is worse than an unbeliever.* Read the context. This passage is about widows within the family. Paul's words are given in the context of an integrated life, not a prioritized life. *Living in faith* involves the integration of all areas of our lives in Jesus. For example, Jesus' followers were guilty of many wrongs according to the religious leaders of that day. His disciples picked grain on the Sabbath,[19] and washed their hands improperly,[20] among other wrongs. Yet in every case, Jesus rebuked their critics.

We need to be careful to discern the difference between our traditions and strategies lest we hold them so dearly that we unwittingly place them before Scripture. There is nothing wrong with keeping traditions or implementing strategies, but we should be careful that we do not elevate them to the same authority as God's Word.[21] Much of today's judgmentalism among Christians occurs because we do this. But that is basically what the Pharisees were doing. God and His book are about living life to the fullest in an integrated manner. We need to be careful that we are not modern-day Pharisees.

As a reminder, Hindus, Buddhists and Muslims teach their followers how to integrate their lives and work better than we do. We separate what they integrate. We need to recalibrate.

Workship

Christians have come to associate "worship" almost exclusively with our weekend gatherings. Worship leaders. Worship teams. Worship style. Worship service. Worship center. None of these terms connects with the work we do the rest of the week. Our church vocabulary creates distance between BOTH work and worship. Perhaps unintentionally, yet the fact remains that we have separated what God's Word joins together. Remember *avodah*? What God's Word joins together we have separated.

Christians have altered the meaning of the word worship. Less than twenty percent of the uses of the word worship in the Bible refer to singing or music. Larry Peabody does the best job of describing the alterations to worship.

> *We've come close to redefining worship as corporate singing. But biblically the word worship does not trace its meaning to music. Bible words translated as worship often describe bodily actions that demonstrate reverence or honor. Old Testament Hebrew words speak of bowing the head, bending the knees or falling prostrate. New Testament words for worship include terms that mean kissing the hand or ground—each requiring one to bow. These terms grew from visible bodily motions that display the unseen worship of the heart or spirit. A. W. Tozer once defined worship as, "A humbling but delightful sense of admiring awe and astonished wonder." Yes, we can express worship through music, but also in many other ways.*
>
> *We've come to see the world as divided into sacred and secular compartments. This way of thinking distorts the way we view work.*

Sacred brings to mind such terms as pure, holy and consecrated. The Merriam-Webster online dictionary even includes the word worship in its definition of sacred: "dedicated or set apart for the service or worship of a deity." All these words describe the kinds of things we know please God. So, if you engage in sacred work, it's easy to think of what you do as a worthy offering as part of your worship. On the other hand, secular gets associated with a completely different set of words. Like worldly. Or profane (the root word of profanity). Or materialistic. One atheistic group calls its website the Secular Web. So, if you think of your work as secular, you won't see much potential for offering it as worship.[22]

Jesus tells us that the kind of worshipers the Father seeks, are those who worship in Spirit and truth.[23]

As we have learned, the Hebrew words *avodah, sharath,* and the Greek words *diakonia, latreias, leitourgias,* though translated at times in our English Bibles as "service" or "ministry," mean much more than that. The New Testament writers were handcuffed in their translating because Greek has no equivalent word for *avodah* or *sharath.* What we need in the English language is a word, God's word, in English, for work, service, and worship. Just because the Greek and English languages have no equivalent doesn't mean we cannot invent a word. The Oxford English Dictionary adds dozens of new words every year. As the world changes so does our vocabulary.

God views work, service, worship as one. So instead of asking people what do you do? Or what is your job, maybe we should be asking, what is your ministry? Or maybe we need a new word altogether—one word that combines work, service and worship. If we start with work, include service, and end with worship we get workserviceworship. Yes, too complicated. If we cut out the middle, we get "workship."

Workship. Workship is work. Workship is service. Workship is worship. On Sundays, Mondays, and every day of the week, I go to workship. Try it out the next time you see a friend, "Hey! How ya doing? How's your workship?"

Another misunderstanding that hinders believers from perceiving work as worship is the idea that in worship we must focus our thoughts exclusively on God. Suppose our job is to repair buildings, plumbing, write a financial report, or drill cavities. Do those jobs divert attention away from God and so cancel any worship? In Exodus 31, God says,

> *I have called by name Bezalel, the son of Uri, the son of Hur, of the tribe of Judah. I have filled him with the Spirit of God in wisdom, in understanding, in knowledge, and in all kinds of craftsmanship, to make artistic designs for work in gold, in silver, and in bronze, and in the cutting of stones for settings, and in the carving of wood, that he may work in all kinds of craftsmanship. And behold, I Myself have appointed with him Oholiab, the son of Ahisamach, of the tribe of Dan; and in the hearts of all who are skillful I have put skill, that they may make all that I have commanded you.*[24]

Is not Bezalel anointed, and called to his job? Does his skill come from his own learning and experience or from God? This is one of several places in the Old Testament where, as it is with the priests, workmen are "set apart," called and anointed by God to do their job—this is workship! Sundays I workship by singing unto the Lord and praising. Monday I workship by working my job unto the Lord and praising.

Summary

The New Testament never labels some work as sacred and other work as secular. In fact, Paul tells us several times: "*Whatever you do, work at it with all your heart, as working for the Lord, not human masters.*"[25] The postmodern world is upon us. We need to recalibrate our evangelistic methodologies and strategies to fit the times. In addition, we need to recognize how harmful and unbiblical some of our "Christian" terms have become. In God's mind there is no male or female, black or yellow, rich or poor, priest or non-priest. We need to recalibrate our words and lose those terms that reflect a "spiritual" hierarchy within His Kingdom.

We need to embrace the future. That means outreach will become less and less about programs and events, and more about validating a person's calling and then working with them to make God's assignment for them become a reality.

What needs to be recalibrated?

- our evangelism
- our terminology
- our attitudes and our hearts

We know that we have come to know him if we keep his commands. Whoever says, "I know him," but does not do what he commands is a liar, and the truth is not in that person. But if anyone obeys his word, love for God is truly made complete in them. This is how we know we are in him: Whoever claims to live in him must live as Jesus did.[26]

11

RECALIBRATING

FOUR LESSONS

If you do what you've always done, you'll get what you've always gotten. —Tony Robbins

I think preachers spend a lot of time, and rightly so, thinking about ancient problems. And while I'm sure people in Bible times wrestled with tough problems, however, our world is very different from theirs.[1] —John Knapp

… and everything that does not come from faith is sin. —Romans 14:23

—————

IT WAS THE PASSOVER. This would be Jesus' last night with the Twelve. He had prepared one final team exercise before surrendering Himself to the authorities. He gathered His disciples together knowing He needed to prepare them for the coming weekend. It was to be a devastating, heart-breaking weekend for them all and full of surprises, but Jesus knew what was coming. His team exercise had four review lessons;[2] four tests that would tie together all His teachings and their experiences together.

Lesson one begins in a most unusual way. Jesus did something that was unheard of at that time; the Teacher fulfills the duty of a lowly slave—He washes the feet of His students.[3] We can imagine that they all argued, trying to stop Him, but only Peter's rebuff is recorded. Yet Jesus persists and then summarizes the activity by stating, *I have set you an example that you should do as I have done for you. Very truly I tell you, no slave is greater than his master, nor is a messenger greater than the one who sent him. Now that you know these things, you will be blessed if you do them.*[4]

Humility, not honor, is God's way. Loving others requires serving others. Jesus demonstrated that His humble example was to be prioritized over cultural traditions. His teachings, actions and words, were to be the standard from then on, and not Jewish cultural rules or religious traditions. Love requires serving. Life in Christ is not about how high you can rise, but how low you are willing to go.

The minds of the disciples are still confused and distraught over Jesus' cultural foot-washing teaching when He moves to lesson two. Jesus provokes their thinking again. *One of you is going to betray me.*[5] Really? You can feel their recoil, their resistance. No way! But one thing they have learned is that Jesus is always right ... so what are they to think?

Lesson two, like lesson one, again reveals the hearts of the disciples. Their attention and concern quickly focuses on themselves. "Is it I?" And, if that's not enough, as soon as Judas's betrayal is exposed, the disciples begin focusing on who among them would become the greatest in heaven![6] For three years they had walked with Jesus, yet their thoughts remained centered on themselves and not on Jesus and doing His will. Though they were His closest followers, they were revealing just how self-centered they were.

Lesson three begins as the disciples gather to celebrate the Passover meal. The Passover meal is one of the most sacred holidays in the Jewish calendar. Families gather in observance of God's Passover covenant to give thanks and remember His faithfulness upon their ancestors' exit from Egypt.

Several of the disciples had worked all day. The room was arranged, the food prepared and served. The meal begins and all are enjoying the feast when Jesus pauses and speaks. Time for lesson three. Jesus ties His previous humility and servitude to the sacrifice of the Passover lamb, which represents His own body and blood. He is positing what He will soon model—the laying down of His own life for others. Jesus is our teacher. Jesus is God; life is not about us. Humility, servanthood, sacrifice is each modeled and verbalized during this final evening together. Now it is time to die … to self. The Passover covenant, He declares, will soon be fulfilled and a new covenant released. Jesus tells them, *A new command I give you: Love one another. As I have loved you, so you must love one another. By this everyone will know that you are my disciples, if you love one another.*[7]

Jesus' last hours without chains, were invested with His Father praying in the garden. His relationship with God was personal and He invites us to have that same personal relationship with God. Yet relationships are fluid, no two relationships are the same. However, the leaders of Israel had designed processes and written rules for the people to follow in order to obey God. There was a "prescribed way" of seeking God. That is, the people did not worship God according to His way, but rather they worshipped Him in their own way. And even though the Twelve had been with Jesus for three years and Jesus had been discipling them, they still did not understand. The disciples, like the religious teachers, had determined that in just a few days they were going to be great—famous. Simple fishermen from the boondocks now on top of the world. Soon they would all be sitting on thrones, basking in their leadership and power! On the contrary, how vastly different would be their reality. In just a few hours they would be surprised and flee for their lives. Humility comes before honor; obedience to God overrules traditions; and dying to self, for Jesus' sake and the sake of others; were all hard lessons to learn. Yet one final lesson remained.

The last lesson is a stern reminder that Jesus' disciples are being sent out into the world.[8] Persecution is coming. Having been warned and having had time to prepare, under pressure they will still flee and fail the tests of sacrifice and service, faithfulness and perseverance. It is an understatement to say, "Becoming and living as a slave to others is not easy." Disciples, past and present, need to grasp the importance of prayer—intimacy with Jesus—without it we cannot hope to endure the tests and persecutions that are promised to come.[9]

The coming Kingdom is not about us. Jesus is the Passover lamb, the final sacrifice for all sins. Humility, love, sacrifice, and service are every disciple's assignment, and persecution is imminent. That's a lot to take in for one meal. Yet in these four lessons, Jesus gave them enough insight to stay the course and to be ready for what was coming. He laid the three-tiered foundation upon which they could and would build:

1. Communion with God
2. Prayer
3. Love—serving one another and putting others before themselves.

LOVE one another. PRAY for one another. PRAYER and LOVE in relationship with God are His keys for opening hearts and releasing His power among all peoples.

Takeaways

What can we learn from Jesus' final lessons, from the disciples and even from the religious leaders of that day? Paul writes to the church in Corinth, *knowledge puffs up, but love builds up*.[10] Are there things we need to reconsider and recalibrate? As you read these pages, what is the Holy Spirit saying to you?

Rather than tear others down, we steadfastly focus on the upward prize in Christ Jesus. We live for the sole purpose of dying.[11] We yearn for His power to work through prayer and love.[12] We run to win, to obtain the prize.[13] We will reach one person at a time with practical know-how, with holistic effort and with passion. Our goal, simply put, is His glory among all peoples. We yearn to join in that *great multitude that no one can count, from every nation, tribe, people and language, standing before the throne and in front of the Lamb; wearing white robes and holding palm branches, crying out for eternity, "Salvation belongs to our God, who sits on the throne, and to the Lamb."*[14]

We are, however, championing the changing of our mission thinking and applications. Our objective is to deliver more than just words to our present and future brothers and sisters. We desire to help one another integrate our life, work and worship into—*workship*. Our objective is to achieve His revealed purposes so that we live out His commands in His power and His knowledge.

We know our lives in Jesus are one. God does not compartmental-ize; we are one body. We are one in Him. The right information brings knowledge, and knowledge yields influence. Our task is to exhort one another to maximize our gifts, talents and experiences for Jesus' glory. Sharing it is empowerment. We understand that as important as ideas are, *the Kingdom of God does not consist of talk, but of power.*[15]

God has commanded us to reach all peoples: the guy in the next desk, the gal across the counter. Business is about people. Business-based outreach allows us to walk with people in *their* journey of life. To love our neighbor is to be present with them in good times and bad. It means placing the needs and goals of our co-workers and neighbors above our own. It entails dying to self and setting aside our own agenda that we may walk with them and help them achieve theirs. Prayer and love are selfless acts that flow from the heart: they are not strategies found on lists of effective management techniques. They are difficult to apply in our daily life and work. Prayer and love require extra time and are difficult to measure. Yet if we are to shine His Light, we need prayer and love to help us reflect the values of God's kingdom. If we are to serve and win others, we have to recalibrate our attitudes and practices, redesign our human tools and strategies and retrain our people. That is a lot to recalibrate!

The very moment you separate body and spirit, you end up with a corpse. I believe that if you separate faith and works, you get the same thing—a corpse. My prayer is that this book will challenge the way you see the world and your work in it. I hope it encourages you in your walk with Jesus and shakes up your paradigms of ministry—I mean workship. Martin Luther sparked the Protestant Reformation. God has shown many of us that once again there is a need for new thinking. Scripture and reason convince us that the church needs new paradigms for these new times.

We need to recalibrate. Recalibrate leadership, training, education, sending, all of which will be covered in the next books of the Workship series. And in recalibrating, I want to be bold, yet receptive to counsel. Where I am wrong, I ask that you show me through Scripture or reasoning. Appeal to my conscience. Be like the Bereans and *examine the scriptures daily to see if these things are so.*[16]

In short, our message need not be acceptable to everyone and neither do we need to strive for political correctness. We are not seeking greater security, nor are we avoiding persecution. Reaching the world through the marketplace is not about watering down our global mandate, neither does it affirm a naive transparency that lacks prudence. And above all, it is definitely not about getting rich in a worldly way.

What does it mean to make His message understandable? It means living out Jesus' words under His authority and with His power. Following Jesus in the 21st century means living an integrated life. As we follow Jesus in today's world, it means we are fully aware of the profound impact that globalization, terrorism, pluralism and science have on the way people live, think, and minister. If we are going to make an impact for Jesus, we need to 'get real' and allow Him to live in and through us 24/7. Tackling the complexities of the 21st century requires actions more than words. Words are extremely important; yet with all the fake news, actions speak louder than words. We need a holistic view of life and work—worship. We need to be incarnational. We need to embody the Good News of Jesus in everything we do and everywhere we go, especially in our places of work.

It's Time to Recalibrate

It is often said that change is the only constant in life, yet people are predisposed to resist change because of the risk associated with it. In spite of the inclination toward resistance, we need to recalibrate. Getting things right—God's right—is as important as ever.

Napoleon once said, *One must change one's tactics every ten years if one wishes to maintain one's superiority.* Today, the pace of change is immensely faster and it will only continue to accelerate. In every area of life and work today, we accept that organizations and people who do not embrace change are bound to lose ground and thus stagnate. The Gospel is clear: work and worship are to be integrated—not because it is a good strategy, but because it is God's strategy.

Every strategy devised to share the Gospel is good. And if prayer and love are involved, every strategy works. However, no evangelistic strategy is as natural and creates more time with people than working with them. If the unreached are to both hear and experience God's grace, forgiveness and love, there is no better way to do that than to work alongside them. But to alter our strategies we need to alter our ways of thinking. If we recalibrate and change, to a business-based model of outreach. This will require a lot of personal growth, especially among those who we call "clergy." It may also require time. We may have to grow in our knowledge of business and leadership. We may need a completely different level of cultural understanding to operate in the workplace world of those we are trying to reach. We will definitely need the Holy Spirit constantly revealing to us the areas where we are not allowing His love to shine through in our actions and words. All of this will take time and demand a lot, but I guarantee that when we workship the Lord in our places of work, we will discover a fresh new depth in our relationship with God.

The first step toward recalibrating is understanding. I pray this book has brought you a better understanding of God's will and revealed to you a new and different way to approach making disciples of all the nations, including those you work with each day. The cost of doing things our ways—the ways we have been doing them for centuries—is far higher than the price of change.

It is not our tools and strategies that are at stake, but God's glory.

It is Him we proclaim, warning every man and teaching every man so that we may present every man mature in Christ.[17]

TERMINOLOGY

BAM (*Business as Mission*): Business as mission is demonstrating what the Kingdom of God is like in the context of business—and as we do so, engaging with the world's more pressing social, economic, environmental, and spiritual issues. Business as Mission involves profitable and sustainable businesses who are intentional about sharing the Kingdom of God while focused on holistic transformation and the multiple bottom lines of economic, spiritual, social, and environmental impact. Business as mission is a concept that can and should be applied everywhere, but the business as mission movement has a special concern for people and places where there are dire economic, social, environmental, and spiritual needs.

BAMer (*Business as Mission worker*): A person who is doing business as mission.

B4T (*Business for Transformation*): Business for Transformation is a subset of Business of Mission that brings eternal impact to the least reached through wealth generating businesses. A B4T business is a business strategically placed in an unreached area (10/40 Window) that is striving for profitability and designed to create jobs and bless the local community in Jesus' name, generally through transformation and specifically through evangelism, discipleship, and church planting. B4T is a subset of BAM, in that BAM is worldwide and B4T is focused on the Muslim, Hindu, and Buddhist peoples of the world.

B4Ter (*Business for Transformation worker*): A person who is doing B4T.

Transformation: Referring to impacting a community in four measurable ways: spiritually, economically, socially, and environmentally.

NGO (**Non-Governmental Organization**): An organization that is not government sponsored but is a non-profit charity. (Many mission organizations have multiple NGOs that do a variety of services such as providing medical services, education, job training, or giving aid to the poor. Many micro-enterprise development projects are also NGOs.)

OPEN: A network of hundreds of B4Ters living and working in the 10/40 Window.

Platform: Often refers to a business identity used by a worker/missionary as a means of legitimizing his or her presence and work among people in limited access contexts. In many cases these businesses are paper fronts or do not produce a profit. The worker is heavily dependent on donor funds.

10/40 Window: A band encompassing Saharan and Northern Africa and almost all of Asia (West Asia, Central Asia, South Asia, East Asia and much of Southeast Asia). (Roughly two-thirds of the world's population lives in the 10/40 Window.) This Window is populated by people who are predominantly Muslim, Hindu, Buddhist, Animist, Jewish, or Atheist.

———

I alone cannot change the world, but I can cast a stone across the waters to create many ripples. —Mother Teresa

ACKNOWLEDGMENTS

My goal in both seeking and writing has been to strive with all my heart, soul, mind, and strength to gain some clarity of what the Father sees, feels, and senses; so I may experience His fullness of truth, joy, and wisdom. My main source of guidance in this is the Bible, so my objective in writing this book is to help people think biblically in a way that brings lasting change. All permanent change takes place by altering how a person perceives reality, so this is an attempt from Scripture, to share what I believe is Jesus' perspective on reality.

For fifty years, I have been committed to seeing Jesus' name uplifted among every tribe, people, language, and nation. Matthew 24:14 has been foundational in igniting my wife's and my assignment in striving to lay down our lives for His glory:

"And the Good News about the Kingdom will be preached throughout the whole world, so that all nations will hear it, and then, finally, the end will come."

My wife, May, plays an integral part in everything I do. For forty years, we have done almost everything together. We love the journey the Lord has put us on but it has not been an easy road. Thank you, May, for your perseverance in journeying with me.

I have the privilege of working with hundreds of Business for Transformation workers (B4Ters) around the world. Their commitment to walk with Jesus in difficult places inspires me. Their experiences in B4T, both challenge and sharpen my thoughts. Without them, this book would lack substance. To all of you in the OPEN network, thank you!

There were many wonderful people involved in bringing this book together. Abby, Arnold, Bethany, Dick, Gary, Heidi, Holli, Leslie and Lud. THANK YOU for your hours of editing! Heidi and Bethany, I am asking Jesus to give you an additional jewel in your crown for all the work you have done to get the copy ready. However, please don't put your marking pens away yet: there are a couple more books to go!

Over twenty B4T workers in the OPEN network contributed stories and ideas, most of them not wishing to be named.

And the entire OPEN staff gave me time and encouragement.

THANK YOU to all of you!

NOTES

Preface

1. Joshua 5:13-14
2. Psalm 58:1
3. 2 Timothy 3:17
4. Acts 17:11
5. Christianity Today. June 13, 2019 https://www.christianitytoday.com/ct/2019/june-web-only/apology-christian-99-1-percent-lausanne-gwf-michael-oh.html
6. John 14:6

1. Recalibrating

1. https://www.pewresearch.org/fact-tank/2017/04/06/why-muslims-are-the-worlds-fastest-growing-religious-group/
2. https://www.pewresearch.org/fact-tank/2017/04/06/why-muslims-are-the-worlds-fastest-growing-religious-group/
3. Matthew 13:8
4. http://www.thetravelingteam.org/stats
5. ibid.
6. Matthew 24:14
7. Revelation 7:9
8. Matthew 24:12
9. Matthew 24:14 NIV
10. Acts 24:16; Philippians 2:15
11. PAGAN CHRISTIANITY – Exploring the Roots of our Church Practices. by Frank Viola & George Barna. Tyndale House Publishers Carol Stream IL, 2008 p. xxv
12. Matthew 24:14
13. https://www.joshuaproject.net/people_groups/statistics
14. Revelation 5:9&10; 7:9
15. Luke 14:25-34
16. Matthew 24:36; Acts 1:7
17. Hot, Flat and Crowded – Why We Need A Green Revolution And How It Can Renew America. By: Thomas L. Friedman. Farrar, Straus and Giroux, New York, 2008 p. 65
18. https://www.prb.org/populationtrendsandchallengesinthemiddleeastandnorthafrica/
19. Revelation 5:9, 7:9-10; 11:9; 13:7; 14:6
20. OPEN is a network of network of 140+ businesses and involving hundreds of B4T workers doing business exclusively among Hindus, Buddhists and Muslims, where there are few or no churches. OPEN's passion is to glorify God by inspiring, connect-

ing, and nurturing B4Ters – one person, and one business at a time. See www.OPENworldwide.net .

21. Business for (4) Transformation. A business strategically placed in an unreached area designed to create jobs and bless the local community in Jesus' name, generally through transformation and specifically through evangelism, discipleship, and church planting.
22. 1 Corinthians 4:12
23. 1 John 3:18
24. James 2:14

3. Recalibrating Our Approaches to People

1. Matthew 23:37
2. Ecclesiastes 12:12 AMP
3. Ecclesiastes 12:13 AMP
4. Acts 26:24
5. 1 Corinthians 8:1b-3
6. Philippians 2:12
7. Hebrews 11:6
8. Galatians 5:16
9. 2 Corinthians 10:5
10. Ephesians 5:32
11. Colossians 1:26-27
12. 1 Corinthians 13:11
13. Matthew 18:2-3
14. 1 Corinthians 13:12
15. Sheldon, Charles. In His Steps, Chicago Advance, Chicago, IL. 1896. p.76
16. https://www.macmillandictionary.com/us/dictionary/american/business
17. Colossians 3:23
18. Genesis 1:27-28
19. Luke 16:9
20. https://www.investopedia.com/ask/answers/13/what-is-non-government-organization.asp and https://en.wikipedia.org/wiki/Non-governmental_organization
21. Genesis 1:27-28; 2:15
22. John 13:35
23. Matthew 12:13-14
24. Luke 8:43-48
25. Luke 19:5-9
26. John 5:1-17
27. Matthew 19:13-15
28. Matthew 15:22-28
29. Mark 6:35-43
30. Luke 10:31-32
31. Colossians 3:17
32. Matthew 22:37-39

4. Recalibrating Our View Of God's View ... Of Work

1. Colossians 3:17
2. Englishman's Concordance http://biblehub.com/hebrew/leavedah_5647.htm
3. Ibid.
4. Colossians 3:17
5. Dave Huber, https://www.efcatoday.org/story/avodah-word-study
6. Ira F. Stone, "Service is Work and Work is Worship" at http://www.ritualwell.org/blog/service-work-and-work-worship-rabbi-ira-f-stone (accessed August, 29, 2016).
7. Genesis 1:28
8. Silvoso, Ed. *Anointed for Business*, 2009 p. 44.
9. Matthew 5:48
10. Psalm 8:1-4, 19:1; Romans 1:20; Colossians 1:16
11. The root word *sharath* שָׁרַת means "to serve" or "ministry." In Genesis 39:4, and 1 Kings 1:15 and in twenty other places *sharath* שָׁרַת is translated as a verb "to attend" or "to serve," and as a noun as "attendant" or "servant." The word *sharath* reflects working or serving. The word in 1 Kings 1:15 (and Genesis 39:4; Genesis 40:4; Numbers 3:6; Deuteronomy 39:4; 2 Kings 4:43; 2 Kings 6:15; 2 Samuel 13:17,18; 1 Kings 10:5; 2Chronicles 9:4; Esther 2:2; Esther 6:3; 1 Kings 1:4,15) usually refers to a higher level of work or service being done for a leader or for royalty.

    This word *sharath* שָׁרַת is also used in reference to acts of special service in spiritual worship. Over forty times *sharath* is translated as "ministry or minister or serve" in reference to acts done on behalf of God before the people of Israel. (Some examples: Exodus 28:35; 2 Chronicles 13:10; Joel 1:9,13; Joel 2:17; 1 Kings 8:11 2Chronicles 5:14; Deuteronomy 17:12; Deuteronomy 21:5; Jeremiah 33:21; Isaiah 61:6.)

    Specifically, it is used in reference to the Levites, the Aaronic priests and their service or ministry to God. (Some examples: Numbers 3:6; Numbers 8:26; Numbers 18:2, 1ʹ Chronicles 15:2; 2 Chronicles 29:11 Numbers 16:9; 1 Chronicles 16:4; 2 Chronicles 23:6; 29:11; Ezra 8:17.)
12. Various translations such as the NASB favor the translation "service" more than the NIV or KJV. However, there is evidence that even between the KJV and NIV translations favor an understanding of diakonia that is broader than just doing work, or services (ministry) for the Church.
13. Acts 7:42; Philippians 3:3; Hebrews 10:2
14. Colossians 3:22-24:
15. Work Matters – Lessons from Scripture. Paul R. Stevens. Wm. B. Eerdmans Publishing. 2012 p.134
16. *God At Work*, Gene Edward Veith, Jr., p. 13

5. Deciphering Translation

1. John 1:1
2. Matthew 12:34-37
3. Exodus 35:30-33
4. Acts 16:37

5. Acts 23:6
6. Acts 22:3
7. Acts 26:5
8. Acts 26:10
9. Acts 26:11
10. http://bibleq.net/answer/6626/
11. https://biblehub.com/sermons/auth/farrar/paul's_trade.htm
12. Ibid.
13. *Inheriting the Crown in Jewish Law: The Struggles for Rabbinic Compensation, Tenure and Inheritance Rights*, University of South Carolina. Carolina Press, 2006, p.5
14. Mishnah, *Avot* 4:5.
15. https://www.britannica.com/topic/Pharisee
16. http://bibleq.net/answer/5325/
17. Genesis 4:22
18. 2 Chronicles 2:13
19. Genesis 4:21
20. Exodus 31:6
21. Exodus 36:1
22. 1 Kings 7:13; 2 Chronicles 4:11
23. Ezra 3:8; 5:2
24. Ezra 3:9
25. Proverbs 22:29
26. https://sites.psu.edu/rclperdue/2014/09/19/the-big-three-of-greek-philosophy-socrates-plato-and-aristotle/
27. A short history of translation through the ages by Marie Lebert, version of 21 June 2017.
    https://marielebert.wordpress.com/2016/11/02/translation/
28. In 382AD Pope Damasus commissioned Jerome to create a definitive Latin version of the Bible. This Bible, called the "Vulgate," was completed in 405AD. The Vulgate was the established Bible of the whole Western church until the Reformation in 1517AD. Jerome completed his translation nearly one thousand years before John Wycliffe completed the first English translation of the Bible in 1395AD.
29. 7 Ways Professional Translators Share their Creativity with the World
    Apr 10, 2018 https://www.globalme.net/blog/7-ways-translators-are-creative
30. American Journal of Linguistics. 2014; Vol 3(1): 1-8. 'Why and how the Translator Constantly Makes Decisions about Cultural Meaning" by Bilal Khalid Khalaf. University of Leicester, Leicester UK
31. "Qualitative research and translation dilemmas". SAGE Publications, (London, vol. 4(2) p.168
    BOGUSIA TEMPLE AND ALYS YOUNG, University of Salford and University of Manchester
32. 7 Ways Professional Translators Share their Creativity with the World
    Apr 10, 2018 https://www.globalme.net/blog/7-ways-translators-are-creative
33. https://www.ted.com/talks/
    lera_boroditsky_how_language_shapes_the_way_we_think?referrer=playlist-the_most_popular_ted_talks_of_2018 Lera Boroditsky. "How language shapes the way we think" TEDWomen 2017

34. THE TIMES OF ISRAEL "Scholar's coveted Bible translation, 22 years in the making, set to hit shelves". November 30, 2018 www.timesofisrael.com/scholars-coveted-bible-translation-22-years-in-the-making-set-to-hit-shelves/
35. Isaiah 55:8-9
36. *PAGAN CHRISTIANITY – Exploring the Roots of our Church Practices*, by Frank Viola & George Barna. Tyndale House Publishers, Carol Stream, IL. 2008. p.105
37. 1 Corinthians 13:12
38. Romans 11:25, 16:25; 1 Corinthians 2:7; Ephesians 1:9; Colossians 1:27
39. 2 Corinthians 5:7
40. Matthew 25:23
41. Parables in Matthew: 13 – Wheat & Tares; 18 – Law of Forgiveness; 21 – The Wicked Tenants; 22 – The Marriage Feast; 24 – Faithful and Unfaithful Servants
42. Nancy DeMoss, SURRENDER – The Heart God Controls. p. 72-74
43. Galatians 5:16

6. Lessons On Farming

1. First written in GMI Info magazine, 1997, and copied into my personal notes. Author unknown.
2. Luke 14:28-30
3. Matthew 25:14-30
4. Matthew 13:13-14; Mark 4:12
5. John 15:16
6. Matthew 13:24-30
7. Matthew 13:19
8. Luke 12:12; 21:15
9. John 4:1-42
10. John 13:35 NIV
11. John 8:28, 38; 12:49; 14:10; 15:18-20; 17:8
12. Matthew 10:20
13. 1 John 3:18
14. Matthew 5:43-45 NIV
15. Matthew 5:16
16. Mark 5:1-20
17. Mark 5:19
18. John 16:13
19. 1 Corinthians 3:6
20. Matthew 9:35-37; Luke 10:2
21. Jonah 4:2

7. The Two Plows

1. Hebrews 4:12
2. Mark 9:29
3. Hebrews 11:6b

4. Hebrews 11:1
5. Hebrews 11:6a
6. Mark 9:25
7. Luke 18:1
8. Matthew 9:38
9. 1 Corinthians 2:14, 3:19
10. Matthew 22:36-40
11. John 13:34-35
12. 1 John 3:18
13. Luke 7:19
14. Luke 7:22
15. James 2:17-18
16. Personal email
17. 1 Corinthians 4:20
18. 1 Thessalonians 1:5
19. 1 Corinthians 13:4-7
20. Acts 17:11
21. A poem attributed to Paul Gilbert. I memorized this poem in seminary.
22. Personal prayer letter
23. 1 Corinthians 3:10
24. 1 Corinthians 2:4-5
25. John 13:35
26. Matthew 13:18-23
27. Written by Bethany Lowndes
28. Luke 4:18-19
29. Matthew 11:23; Luke 10:13, 19:37
30. Matthew 7:28-29, 13:54; Mark 2:12, 15:5; Luke 20:26
31. Mark 6:2; Luke 4:36, 19:37
32. Romans 1:11
33. Acts 2:1-41; 8:13; 19:11

8. More on Plowing

1. From the Movie "The Two Popes"
2. Proverbs 4:7
3. Exodus 8:19
4. Matthew 5:15-16
5. 2 Timothy 2:12; Hebrews 12:7; 1 Peter 2:20
6. Hebrews 10:36
7. Genesis 26:12-13
8. 1 Corinthians 3:6

9. Work Revisited, Worship Recalibrated

1. Galatians 5:13; 1 Peter 4:10
2. John 13:34, 15:17; Romans 13:8; 1 Peter 4:8
3. James 5:16
4. Romans 15:14
5. John 14:34-35
6. Acts 2:47b
7. Luke 9:23
8. Galatians 2:20
9. Colossians 3:17
10. 1 Corinthians 3:16
11. Colossians 3:23
12. The Greek translation of the Old Testament from the original Hebrew
13. Philippians 4:18
14. 2 Corinthians 9:12
15. Matthew 5:17
16. 1 Peter 2:9
17. 1 Thessalonians 5:17-18
18. 1 Corinthians 3:16, 6:19-20
19. Hebrews 6:10
20. Hebrews 13:15-16
21. Matthew 28:18-20
22. John 20:21
23. Acts 1:8
24. Philippians 2:12
25. http://www.dictionary.com/browse/work?s=t
26. Ephesians 6:7-8
27. Exodus 16:20
28. https://utmost.org/classic/worship-classic/
29. So let's *'avodah'*: work – worship – serve! http://matstunehag.com/2018/08/13/lets-avodah/

10. New Wineskins For New Wine

1. Mark 2:18
2. Luke 5:36-38
3. http://www.thetravelingteam.org/stats
4. ibid.
5. Luke 5:39
6. Matthew 16:2-3
7. https://www.graduateinstitute.ch/highlights/news/azan-moon-anthropological-jour-ney-central-asia
8. Psalm 69:3-4; Psalm 150:6; Colossians 3:23; 1 Cor. 10:31
9. Matthew 28:19-20

10. Getting Beyond the Numbers Game, By James F. Engel, Christianity Today August 7 , 2000. p. 57
11. 2 Samuel 11:1f
12. https://www.zabanga.us/marketing-communications/an-army-of-one-campaign-accomplishes-its-mission.html
13. ibid.
14. The Great Divide, by Mark Green. Publisher LICC London, 2010 p.11
15. Revelation 3:15-16
16. 1 Peter 2:9
17. Luke 9:62; 2 Timothy 2:4
18. Protection: Isaiah 41:10; 2 Corinthians 4:8-9; 2 Thessalonians 3:3; Provision: Philippians 4:19
19. Mark 2:23-38
20. Mark 7:1-8
21. Matthew 15:3-9
22. Peabody, Larry. Job-Shadowing Daniel Walking the Talk at Work (pp. 155-166). Outskirts Press. Kindle Edition.
23. John 4:23
24. Exodus 31:2-6
25. Colossians 3:23, 3:17; Ephesians 2:10, 6:7;
26. 1 John 2:3-6

11. Recalibrating

1. How the Church FAILS Businesspeople (and what can be done about it), by John C. Knapp. William B. Eerdmans Publishing Company. Grand Rapids, MI 2012 pg. 24
2. Note to the reader. The different Gospels record these lessons in different orders; yet the lessons are the same.
3. John 13:1-11
4. John 13:15-17
5. John 13:21
6. Luke 22:24
7. John 13:35
8. Luke 22:35-37
9. Matthew 10:23; 2 Timothy 3:12
10. 1 Corinthians 8:1
11. Luke 9:23-25
12. John 13:34-35; 1 John 3:11
13. 1 Corinthians 9:24
14. Revelation 7:10
15. 1 Corinthians 4:20
16. Acts 17:11
17. Colossians 1:28

ABOUT THE AUTHOR

Patrick Lai and his family have worked in SE Asia for over thirty seven years. His experience in doing business with Jesus has brought him to understand the meaning of work and worship in the marketplace. He started fourteen businesses in four countries, six of which are still operating. The Lord enabled those he discipled to plant three churches among the Chinese and four among Muslims. He is the founder and leader of a network of business professionals working in fifty of the 10/40 Window countries.

Patrick has a Bachelor's degree in Business, a Master of Divinity, and a Doctorate of Intercultural Studies. Patrick is the author of *Tentmaking – The Life and Work of Business as Missions* and *Business for Transformation – Getting Started.* Currently Patrick and his wife mentor and coach businesspeople working where there are few or no Christians.

Made in the USA
Columbia, SC
14 June 2021